345

P9-CFQ-556

Arnold Weigel

CHRIST AND THE MEANING OF LIFE

CHRIST
and the
MEANING OF LIFE
A Book of Sermons and Meditations

HELMUT THIELICKE

Edited and Translated by
JOHN W. DOBERSTEIN

HARPER & ROW, PUBLISHERS

New York and Evanston

CHRIST AND THE MEANING OF LIFE

Copyright © 1962 by John W. Doberstein
Printed in the United States of America

*All rights in this book are reserved.
No part of the book may be used or reproduced
in any manner whatsoever without written permission except in the case of brief quotations
embodied in critical articles and reviews. For
information address Harper & Row, Publishers,
Incorporated, 49 East 33rd Street,
New York 16, N. Y.*

Library of Congress catalog card number: 62-7304

G-P

Contents

6   *Contents*

Translator's Note

Those who are familiar with the literature of preaching know the series of sermon volumes published over a period of years by a Scottish publisher under the title "The Scholar as Preacher." These volumes of sermons by such preachers as W. M. Macgregor, Theodor Zahn, A. E. Garvie, A. J. Gossip, James Moffat, and James S. Stewart still command the respect and warm appreciation of preachers who continue to wrestle with the task of proclaiming the Word in the words of our day.

I mention this because the phrase "scholar as preacher" leaps into my mind whenever I attempt to characterize the preaching of Helmut Thielicke. This combination of deep scholarly, Biblical, and theological mastery with strong, vividly colorful, pictorial utterance, eschewing the worn cliché and employing the stirring verb and the fascinating picture, the kind of speech that goes straight to the hearer's "personal center," no matter whether he be the "intellectual" or the so-called "common man"—this, both preachers and listeners agree, is what preaching must always strive to be. And the comments of professors of homiletics and preachers of all denominations, in reviews and in scores of letters which have come to me from all over the country, bear out this judgment. Again and again the comment occurs: "This is great preaching!"

The following sermons and addresses, most of them presented over the radio and television, reflect in their varying length the time limits imposed by the circumstances of their delivery. They have been edited and arranged from manuscript materials put at the disposal of the translator by the author. Included are three sermons on parables which, for reasons beyond our control, were omitted from *The Waiting Father*, the volume of sermons on the parables of Jesus. It may be noted that the sequence of the sermons and meditations follows the general order of the church year. The following classification of chapters may be found helpful: Advent: 1, Christmas: 2-4, New Year: 5-6, Lent: 7-8, Easter: 9-10, Pentecost: 11, Trinitytide: 12-28. The collection has the distinction of being published in English before appearing in print in the author's native country.

I wish to express here my appreciation to Dr. Thielicke for the confidence he has been willing to repose in me in the task of editing and translating these materials.

JOHN W. DOBERSTEIN

Mount Airy, Philadelphia
October, 1961

CHRIST AND THE MEANING OF LIFE

❧ 1 ☙

World History and World Judgment

How often we are tormented by the thought of all the injustice that occurs in history. How often it is the heaviest battalions that win and not justice. How can one explain the fact that such a diabolical system as Bolshevism is apparently able to maintain itself and is not flung into the abyss by a higher hand? How can we allow this to happen? Again and again the anxious question obtrudes itself. Is the history of the world, as Schiller said, really the judgment of the world? Or is it not, as Theodor Lessing put it, that which gives meaning to the meaningless? But if there are no divine judgments in history, can there be any God at all?

Now, the fact is—and the experience of the men of the Bible confirms it—that the judgments of God simply cannot be established objectively. An example will illustrate this. The song about the shattered armies of Napoleon in Russia declares: "With man and horse and caisson the Lord of hosts did smite them." Is this really a clear case of a judgment of God upon Napoleon? Perhaps a Frenchman might fairly argue that it was just the other way round, that Europe and not Napoleon was the power smitten by God, since it was surely Europe that was in this way deprived of its Napoleonic principle of order and its benefits. And in this judgment was not Napoleon a mere executor of the judgment? Not only is the character of great figures ambiguous in world history; the role assigned to them by divine governance is obviously equivocal.

Then too, when it comes to the unusual events, distresses, and disasters in our personal life, our diagnosis that these are "judgments of God" is always running into an ultimate limit which makes it questionable: Must the suffering I am subjected to when I have an incurable cancer necessarily be attributed to a previously committed sin and therefore be interpreted as a judgment of God? May it not also be possible to explain it on the basis of its purpose, namely, God's educative purpose, and would not these two interpretations of this suffering cancel each other out?

These two interpretations of suffering clash dramatically in Jesus' conversation with his disciples in the story of the man born blind (John 9, especially vss. 1-3). The disciples proceeded from what was to them the self-evident assumption that back of this plight of congenital blindness there must be a sin, that either this man or his parents must have sinned. Jesus rejected this explanation of the disciples and apparently turned it into its opposite. He said that this poor man's blindness served the purpose "that the works of God might be made manifest in him." Accordingly, when afflictions and catastrophes come into our lives, we dare not be content merely to ask, "Why should this happen to me?" but rather, "To what end, for what purpose has this burden been sent to me?"

In any case, it is obviously not a simple matter of establishing a clear connection between suffering and sin.

The fact that we cannot establish a connection between sin and punishment, at least in many cases, that again and again we are thrown back to the question, "Why is God silent, why is he so passive, when we should expect that he would come down in a storm of judgment and set a clear example?"—all this constitutes the severest kind of test of faith precisely for devout people.

But then we must remember that it is by no means true that

when God seems to be silent and passive nothing is happening. The judgment itself may in fact be taking place in his silence and passivity; indeed, his silence and passivity may be the judgment. In the language of faith this means that God withdraws his arm and leaves men to themselves, abandons them to the consequences of their actions and thus delivers them up to their own judgment. The very moments in which the silence of God causes the godless person to feel safe and to mock at such a thing as divine judgment, because he equates the dreadful act of divine permission with the nonexistence of God, can be the very moments when the man of faith sees the judgment of God bearing down upon the world like an oppressive nightmare, so much so that he would actually feel an outburst of an open storm of wrath to be a relief from the weird and sinister oppression of this silent judgment.

We see, therefore, that even the seeming silence of God, his apparent failure to wreak judgment upon the world, cannot be explained by saying that we men lack the antennae to perceive these relationships, or that the impression that God is silent is merely a false acoustical impression produced by our unhearing ears and hardened hearts; as if, in other words, the silence of the Judge were due to the insensitivity of our hearts.

No, the silence of the Judge is an objective thing. It is bound up with the real nature of divine judgment. Even the angels who stand about the throne of God can testify that God's silence is real; so far is it from being merely a figment of man's deluded and hardened heart. God really can be silent. He by no means judges merely—or better, he hardly ever judges, by smiting the transgressor with a stroke of lightning or some other disaster; on the contrary he judges him by letting him go in silence. Thus he allowed the people who built the tower of Babel to wreck themselves on their own godlessness. By doing what seemed to be nothing, he allowed the dispersion to fall upon them in their godlessness. So his silence, far from being passivity, was actually extreme activity. What he allowed to happen there was the equivalent of his coming down and confusing their language. God

was at work in their self-confusion merely by reason of his standing aside and looking on. So he also "gave up" the heathen to
their own ungodliness (Rom. 1:18 ff.).

This giving up and abandonment (*paredoken*) is the way of
silent judgment, though at first sight one might think that here
was an instance in which the law of retribution was apparent to
everybody.

We therefore begin to understand why it is that it is so difficult
to establish a connection between guilt and retribution in history.
And the truth is that one must know the Judge in order to understand his judgments. So long as we do not face this Judge as a
personal Thou who reveals himself as our Father in Jesus Christ,
we shall be hopelessly at the mercy of this question of how the
world order functions. And our situation is actually "hopeless"
in the strict sense, not only because the tormenting question
"Why?" never ceases, but also because it never finds a solution,
because it remains "unredeemed."

The great representative forms of this failure to find a solution, and the redemption that comes with it, generally take one
of two directions:

Either the question "Why?" ends up against a stone wall, the
bleak and comfortless conclusion that the whole thing is unfathomable, from which the next step is the nihilistic conclusion
that the seemingly unfathomable has no basis at all and that therefore the world has no direction and is utterly fatherless.

Or the question "Why?" ends in the conclusion that the whole
thing is nothing more than ice-cold mechanical laws and the
utter silence of nature. A combination of the first and the second
answers is found in the attempt to interpret the finite world
"tragically"; in other words, to posit an order which is a fate that
neither gods nor men can question and one never knows who has
ordered it or what purpose it serves. This situation, which no
longer has any understanding of judgment because it has lost the
Judge, is itself judgment.

The deliverance which the message of the Bible proclaims in
the face of this impenetrable problem of meaning, this painful

mystery of history, consists then not in a solution of the question "Why?" but rather in transforming it into the question "Whither?" and "To what end?"

I come back again to the story of the man born blind. The disciples asked, "Why was this man born blind; who sinned?" But Jesus asked, "To what end was this suffering appointed?" and then went on to answer, "that the works of God might be made manifest in him." The question "Why?" is directed backward to the past and seeks to fathom the causes. The answer it wants runs like this: Because of such and such, God did thus and so.

But this answer cannot be found. It is hidden in the counsel of God. The question "Whither?" and "To what end?" is not desirous of this answer, but is comforted in the certitude that we may confidently allow ourselves to be surprised, because we are being guarded and the Midgard serpent is not lurking on the horizon, for the foundation of the world is friendly and fatherly. So the Christian, facing the enigma of history, does not formulate a syllogism but rather says, "Nevertheless I am continually with thee" (Ps. 73:23). For he sees the judgment from the viewpoint of the Judge. And the Judge is none other than the Father, and Jesus Christ has assured us that we can call upon him and be his children.

It is the face of this Judge that will appear at the Last Judgment. Joseph Wittig once said that a man's biography ought really to begin not with his birth but with his death; it can be written only from the point of view of its end, because only from there can the whole of his life in its fulfillment be seen.

So, not until the world's last hour strikes, that hour of the second advent, when faith will see what it has believed and unbelief will be compelled to see what it has not believed—only that last hour of the world will make known the mystery of the meaning of history, the biography of the world.

❧ 2 ☙

Jesus Christ in the Front-line Trenches

When I was bombed out with my family, and on the following
evening walked through the quiet, peaceful streets of a village,
looking for emergency quarters, I had a curious experience. Before this I had often recovered from the sight of ruins and the
heaviness of heart that came at nightfall by sending my imagina-
tion off on a journey. I thought of a peaceful village with cows
coming down the roads to their barns, and people talking about
the harvest and sitting around the lamp in the evening, a place
that was spared the tumult of war. The people said a friendly
"Good evening," the cozy lamplight shone through the chinks
in the black-out curtains, and everything was as I had imagined
it to be. But the longed-for peace would not come into my heart.
I felt ostracized and the idyllic scene was tormenting rather than
tranquilizing.

In the next few days it drove me back to the ruined city and
the people whose faces were still marked by the runes of terror.
There I felt at home. They understood what I had gone through
because they had suffered it themselves. The people in the village
did not understand. To them I was a somewhat disquieting appa-

rition from another, frightening, world. There is nothing more comforting than to have people who understand one. This is what drove many soldiers who had been at the front, and then on their leave enjoyed a good soft bed for a few nights, back to their comrades in the Russian steppe. When a person is pressed hard by dread and terror, then home and fulfillment and the people who are fortunate and have everything—these suddenly become alien.

This also has something to do with the fact that of all people it is the poets who have become the pastors of our time, who do not hand out idyls, fulfillments, and solutions to problems, but rather cry out their dread, their nothingness, and their despair to the world. How else can we explain the fact that people reach out for the poems of Gottfried Benn? The "Song of the Passion" says: Wounds must heal wounds. The wounded seek refuge with the wounded. There they are understood, and that by itself means a lot.

Every year around Christmastime thoughts like these come to me. People strain themselves to the utmost to give themselves and others a few hours of joy. Wishes are fulfilled; we step out of the moment, in which ordinarily we are completely absorbed, and restore connection with our own childhood. We remember our mothers in whose protecting care we once lived, the mothers who told us about the Christ Child and Father Christmas. The hardest men sing touching little songs, and in the soft light of candles our hearts leap up. We seek these hours in the same way that years ago I sought out the quiet, secure little village, in the same way that the Hungarians may yearn for the shores of freedom. And then when the candles burn down, leaving only blackened stumps or nothing at all, there comes a secret feeling of uneasiness: we have to go back behind the counter again in the big store, back to our examinations, the flurry in the office, or a clattering machine. This quiet world around the candles is so different from our ordinary life that we cannot connect the two, and in a short time the brightness vanishes behind us—like the lights of the station when we pass the curve.

But the intent of Christmas is something totally different. The Child in the crib is not an idyl. It is only our love and often our sentimentality which have turned his story into an idyl. The Child was homeless. He was shoved off into a stable. Shortly afterward his parents went out on the road as refugees in order to escape Herod's massacre of the children. Then came the life-long hostility of men; the Child always remained, even after he grew up, a fugitive. His heart trembled under the impact of all the temptations and fears that shake us too. And finally this life ended as it began he was shoved out of the world; he died on a gallows that had the form of a cross. This Man who loved infinitely, and therefore suffered infinitely as he saw men running headlong to their own destruction—they had no use for him. Crib and cross—they are both of the same wood, they are of a piece.

And I believe that all this, with all its terror, is infinitely more comforting than the soft, sweet spirit we seek at Christmas, which afterward leaves only a hung-over, letdown feeling if it is the only thing there is in it. Jesus Christ did not remain at base head-quarters in heaven, receiving reports of the world's suffering from below and shouting a few encouraging words to us from a safe distance. No, he left the headquarters and came down to us in the front-line trenches, right down to where we live and worry about what the Bolsheviks may do, where we contend with our anxieties and the feeling of emptiness and futility, where we sin and suffer guilt, and where we must finally die. There is nothing that he did not endure with us. He understands everything.

Or do we no longer sense how knowing are the features of this face, which the painters lent even the child and which later gazed upon us from the cross? He does not wear the disinterested face of those people who live in the village called "religion" far behind the mountains of the wicked world; he has the eyes of a person who knows his way about the ruins in our life. Wounds must heal wounds. He became one of the wounded because he wanted to be one of us. And therefore that Face does not vanish when the candles go out. For this Figure knows everything: of my loneliness, when I am alone or in the midst of my fellows, of the things in my life that I cannot handle, of the villain who is bedeviling me, of all my fears. For this Companion is with me in the front-line trenches. I can accept everything from his hand, for his hand knows and controls all things. And he lets down the drawbridge by which I can enter the fortress, long since forgotten, where I shall be secure.

Here is One who is waiting and looking for me.

❧ 3 ❧

The Reflection in a Dark Glass

On the bookshelf opposite my desk there hangs a small photograph of which I am very fond. I put it there so that my eye might fall upon it now and then as I work. It is certainly not an objet d'art. Someone had merely snapped a picture of a scene in a Nativity play.

Even the composition of the scene is by no means what one would call good theater. The picture shows a fairly large company of men in long white robes, most of them younger men, moving toward an altar with candles in their hands. At this altar, quite obviously a product of the 1870's and therefore by no means aesthetically pleasing, four men are seen, standing, kneeling, lying prostrate, and gazing in great terror at the approaching company. One of them is holding his hand before his eyes as if he were blinded, another appears to be trying to hide, and a third is making a gesture of capitulation. It is quite clear what is meant here: the white-clad figures are the heavenly choir of angels and the four men at the altar are the weather-beaten, terrified shepherds.

Frequently one of my friends who stops in to see me picks

up the picture and says with some surprise (sometimes because it is in the middle of summer), "Why do you have this picture hanging here?" Usually the visitor is somewhat embarrassed when he asks the question, since tact forbids him to add, "And besides, it's such an ordinary picture—a picture that indicates no artistic appreciation whatsoever."

In these cases I like to keep my visitors guessing for a while. I ask them who they think these people in the picture are. And the strange thing is that almost all of them give the same answer. "Well now, who could they be? In any case, one is struck by the concentrated, almost rapt, expressions on their faces. They are obviously 'in it' heart and soul and it is clear that for them it is far more than a mere play. They are probably people from a Christian congregation." One visitor even said that the picture was possibly taken in a school for deacons or something like it.

Sometimes I can hardly wait until the guessing game is over to set them straight. "You've missed it altogether," I say to them. "But I can understand how you arrived at your guess. These people are really close to the Christmas miracle and have taken it to heart. They are by no means merely *playing* at worship, but are really 'in it.' But these men are neither members of a Christian brotherhood nor of a school for deacons. It is a photograph of a Christmas celebration in a prison. Some time ago I spoke to the prisoners and visited them in their cells. They listened—well, I can only say, like hungry and thirsty men. The prison chaplain then gave me this picture. 'Look at this young fellow here,' the chaplain said. 'He killed his friend in a fight over a wrist watch. Year after year he has always been entrusted with the same part. He kneels before the crib and says:

> I lay in death, in darkest night;
> Thou wert the Sun that brought to me
> My life, my light, my soul's delight.*

I tell you that when you hear these words out of that mouth, it goes right through you.' "

*Stanza three of Paul Gerhardt's Christmas hymn, "I stand beside thy manger bed." (Trans.)

Why has this picture affected me so deeply and why does it affect my visitors in the same way? I ask myself quite self-critically whether what impresses me in it may not be a certain susceptibility to sentimentality and "sobstuff." The gleam of Christmas candles and the tender festival of love in contrast with murderers and thugs dressed up as angels—this melodrama may be closer to the "tearjerker" novelists than to Luke the evangelist. But I am afraid that, if I were to make such a snobbish judgment, I should be merely trying to dismiss something that actually touched me at a much deeper level, something that touched my heart (and by no means merely my nervous system!).

For this is the miracle which is caught in this picture. Here are men walking out of a dark and murky past to the manger, and the light of Christmas falls upon their bungled lives. But as it falls upon them, it transforms them and makes them shine. For though they come from locked cells and afterward will return to life under lock and key, they are now permitted to stand beneath the heaven which is open and unbarred. I learned from not a few of them that, like the prodigal son, they turned about-face among the swine, that they learned to believe in this blessed light and became new men. Now they are no longer acting a play; they are in dead earnest. Nor are they merely reciting some verses which have been drummed into them; they are confessing their faith. And when this young man says, "I lay in death, in darkest night; thou wert the Sun that brought to me my life . . . ," this *is* a miracle.

Some of you may be thinking: This is a bitter pill he is asking us to swallow. Certainly convicts should have pastoral care and, as far as I am concerned, their Christmas celebrations too, in order that they may examine themselves. But to put me, a serious, decent citizen, on the same level with them, this is stretching what you call being a Christian too far.

And it would in fact be wrong and also quite out of accord with the Christian gospel to wipe out all distinctions between the gifted and the stupid, the competent and the failures, the honest people and the rogues. The concern here is with something else altogether, and I shall try to express it in two different thoughts.

The *first* is that God comes to us at Christmas down in the depths. I do not need to have some kind of religious feelings or to have accomplished something inwardly or outwardly in order to have him come to me. He comes to the stable, to the comfortless, the sick, and the despairing; he walks with the fugitives on the long refugee road, and when my last hour comes and all else forsakes me, I shall be able to say, "When I depart, O Lord, depart thou not from me." For he came down even to the dark valley of death. Crib and cross are both of the same wood.

And then the *second* thing. At some point in our lives every single one of us is poor. This may perhaps not be seen on the outside at all, for we men know very little about one another. I may have a worry on my mind, I may have committed a wrong and feel the burden of guilt, or I may be sick, or scourged by consuming desires that are never fulfilled. The convicts in the photograph represent this side of me. What in me is a hidden darkness has erupted to the surface in them. In that darkness there was no light, only black pits, labyrinths, and hopeless dead-end streets. But now the reflection of *another* light shines upon their faces. Long before they began to ask whether there was still any hope and meaning in their lives, Someone was already on his way to them. Christmas tells us that God comes to find us no matter where we are. And when it seems that everything has come to a dead end, then God's chance really begins.

❧ 4 ☙

The Festival of Light

Though Christmas is the festival of light and is celebrated with many lights, it often seems to me that for us it is not much more than a shadow—the shadow of a Figure who has long since passed by.

It is true, of course, that even the cast shadow has in it a certain greatness. At any rate, it indicates the contours of a reality which even the unsentimental "man of today," who prides himself upon his objectivity, somewhat shamefacedly calls love. At Christmas we are kind to one another, we emphasize the element of community, and enjoy ourselves. The antagonisms that keep thrusting themselves upon us are walled off for a few moments with air cushions, and for a short time the gentle law of kindness reigns.

This may sound ironical—and yet I have just said that even this cast shadow has some greatness in it. Well, both the irony and the greatness are true in their own way. The *greatness* becomes evident when we consider what a miracle it is after all that these images of the shepherds, mother Mary seeking shelter, and the humble stable should be capable of transforming our

24

whole point of view for even a few moments, that they should draw us out of the vicious circle of our daily routine and make us think of our suffering, forsaken, needy fellow men.

For a few moments we are troubled by the thought that anybody should be obliged to spend Christmas Eve without its lights on the lonely sea, that anybody should be walking the streets alone with nothing and nobody to call his own, not even a future. It is the greatness of this shadow that can arouse such sadness and concern.

But the *irony*, or better, the sadness that escapes into irony, appears when we measure the shadow by the original Figure who cast it.

For what is a love that no longer emanates from immediate contact with him who "is" love, but lives in us only as a kind of memory, a mere distant echo? Our everyday speech is sometimes capable of reducing this bizarre shadow of a vanished love and a fleeting joy to a grotesque caricature. I often think how absurd it is for us to say, "Have sunshine in your heart!" or "Wake up happy in the morning!" It is pathetic to see the yearnings that these expressions betray, but at the same time it is quite foolish to put them in the form of imperatives. How can I possibly go about getting the sun into my heart? Obviously, the sun can be there in my heart only if it shines upon me and then the brightness in my heart is a reflection of it. But how in the world can I "produce" the sun?

A person who invents imperatives like these strikes me as being someone who has lost the real thing and finds himself walking around in the darkness where he is compelled to vegetate without love and without joy. So he says to himself: "I cannot live without these basic elements of human life; therefore I must produce them synthetically, namely, by an act of my will." So he summons his heart to produce the sun. The futility of such an attempt is like the fool's trying to catch sunlight in a sack.

When I am asked why as a Christian I celebrate Christmas, my first reply is that I do so because here something has happened *to* me and therefore—but only as I am receptive and give myself to it—something now can happen *in* me.

There is a Sun "that smiles at me," and I can run out of the dark house of my life into the sunshine(as Luther once put it). I live by virtue of the miracle that God is not merely the mute and voiceless ground of the universe, but that he comes to me down in the depths. I see this in him who lay in the manger, a human child, and yet different from us all. And even though at first I look upon it only as a lovely colored picture, seeing it with the wondering eyes of a child, who has no conception whatsoever of the problem of the personhood of God and the Trinity and the metaphysical problems of time and eternity, I see that he, whom "all the universe could not contain," comes down into the world of little things, the little things of *my* life, into the world of homelessness and refugees, a world where there are lepers, lost sons, poor old ladies, and men and women who are afraid, a world in which men cheat and are cheated, in which men die and are killed. Crib and cross: these are the nethermost extreme of life's curve; no man can go any deeper than this; and he traversed it all. I do not need first to become godly and noble before I can have part in him. For there are no depths in my life where he has not already come to meet me, no depths to which he has not been able to give meaning by surrounding them with love and making them the place where he visits me and brings me back home.

Once it *happened, once* in the world's history it happened, that someone came forward with the claim that he was the Son of God and the assertion "I and the Father are one," and that he proved the legitimacy of that claim, not by acting like a supernatural being or stunning men with his wisdom or communicating knowledge of higher worlds, but rather by proving his claim through the depths to which he descended. A Son of God who defends his title with the argument that he is the brother of even the poorest and the guilty and takes their burden upon himself: this is a fact one can only note, and shake one's head in unbelief—or one must worship and adore. There is no other alternative. I must worship. That's why I celebrate Christmas.

What then is the good of all the usual religious froth? What do these pious sentimentalities actually accomplish? Aren't they really "opium"? What difference does it make if I see in God the Creator of the galaxies and solar systems and the microcosm of the atom? What is this God of macrocosm and microcosm to me if my conscience torments me, if I am repining in loneliness, if anxiety is strangling me? What good is that kind of a God to me, a poor wretch, a heap of misery, for whom nobody cares, whom people in the subway stare at without ever seeing?

The "loving Father above the starry skies" is up there in some monumental headquarters while I sit in a foxhole somewhere on this isolated front (cut off from all communication with the rear), somewhere on this trash heap, living in lodgings or a mansion, working at a stupid job that gives me the miseries or at an executive's desk which is armored with two anterooms . . . what do I get out of it when someone says, "There is a Supreme Intelligence that conceived the creation of the world, devised the law of cause and effect, and maneuvered the planets into their orbits?" All I can say to that is, "Well, you don't say so! A rather bold idea, but almost too good to be true," and go on reading my newspaper or turn on the television. For that certainly is not a message by which I could live.

But if someone says, "There is Someone who knows you, Someone who grieves when you go your own way, and it cost him something (namely, the whole expenditure of life between the crib and the cross!) to be the star to which you can look, the staff by which you can walk, the spring from which you can drink"—when someone says *that* to me, then I prick up my ears and listen. For if it is true, *really* true, that there is Someone who is interested in me and shares my lot, then this can suddenly change everything that I hoped for and feared before. This could mean a revolution in my life, at any rate a revolution in my judgment and knowledge of things.

In other words, I should say that all the atheists, nihilists, and agnostics are right at *one* point, and that is when they say that the course of history gives us no basis whatever for any knowledge of God and the so-called "higher thoughts" that govern our world. But Christmas teaches us that, if we wish to know God, we must in our relationship to the world begin at a completely *different* end, namely, that we do not argue from the structure of the world to God, but rather from the Child in the manger to the mystery of the world, to the mystery of *the* world in which the manger exists. For if this Child exists, then he is the heart and center of the world, then, to put it in philosophical terms, he is the hermeneutical principle which unlocks the mystery of the world.

Then I see in this Child that in the background of this world there is a Father. I see that love reigns above and in the world, even when I cannot understand this governance, and I am tormented by the question of how God can permit such tragic things to happen. (This problem confronts us even at this heart and center of the world; for how could God allow his beloved Son to be born in a stable, how could he allow him to die on the gallows, how could the Lord of the world be driven out of the world, how could there be a darkness which could not be overcome?)

But if the manifestation of love conquers me at *one* point, namely, where Jesus Christ walked this earth and loved it, then I can trust that it will also be the message at those points in the story of life which I cannot understand. Even a child knows that his father is not playing tricks on him when he refuses to grant one of his wishes and thus treats him in a way that is seemingly incompatible with love. The highest love is almost always incognito and therefore we must trust it.

So even for the Christian the mysteries of life are by no means solved so far as his reason and understanding is concerned. But as a disciple I can have the peace which passes all understanding and which therefore cannot be shaken by reason either, because it is itself allied with it.

Let me put it in the form of an illustration. If I look at a fine piece of fabric through a magnifying glass, I find that it is perfectly clear around the center of the glass, but around the edges it tends to become distorted. But this does not mislead me into thinking that the fabric itself is confused at this point. I know that this is caused by an optical illusion and therefore by the way in which I am looking at it. And so it is with the miracle of knowledge which is bestowed upon me by the Christmas event: If I see the world through the medium of the Good News, then the center is clear and bright. There I see the miracle of the love that descends to the depths of life. On the periphery, however, beyond the Christmas light, confusion and distortion prevail. The ordered lines grow tangled and the labyrinthine mysteries of life threaten to overwhelm us. Therefore our sight, which grows aberrant as it strays afield, must recover its perspective by returning to the thematic center. The extraordinary thing is that the mystery of life is not illuminated by a formula, but rather by another mystery, namely, the News, which can only be believed and yet is hardly believable, that God has become man and that now I am no longer alone in the darkness.

That's why I celebrate Christmas.

❦ 5 ❦

Time and Eternity

Before it strikes twelve on New Year's Eve we shall all be keeping our eyes glued to the clock. But this gaze will be different from the quick look we take at our wrist watch to see if we shall get to an appointment on time or to see whether the train has already left. On this last night of the old year when we look at the clock we shall have a rather special and hard-to-define feeling. At other times we use the clock in order to move according to what it says, in order to be at such and such a place on time. But on New Year's Eve we do not move at all; we sit in the company of friends or perhaps in a room by ourselves. Then, suddenly, it is time, instead of us, that moves. The last minutes of the old year have come. And for a moment we hear the stream of time, which is otherwise so noiseless, beginning to murmur aloud as it plunges over the weir of this out-of-the-ordinary midnight. One must be very blasé or very stupid if one does not feel a little shiver going down one's back when it happens. Why is it that on this night we have this completely different sense of time?

I should like to suggest what may seem at first to be a rather surprising reason for this. The reason why we experience time so utterly differently in this midnight hour than we do at other times lies in the fact that our clocks are round! Naturally I shall have to substantiate this statement. Because our clocks are round, because the hands circle about and constantly return to their starting point, we acquire the illusion that everything in life repeats itself, that we can always make a fresh start. What I have not done today by six o'clock I will get done tomorrow by six o'clock. In other words, the hand on my clock will make its circle tomorrow just as it did today. On the last night of the year, however, we experience time in a different way. Then all at once time no longer moves in a circle, but in a straight line. There are no such things as round "year-clocks" which begin afresh at number twelve after the passage of three hundred and sixty-five days. We should have to visualize such a yearly chronometer quite differently; it would have to be a straight line on which every elapsed year was marked off as a small segment. And all our life we creep along this line of time. We leave behind us one segment after another. The hand never returns to where it was before. Once decisions are made we can never cancel them out.

In some past segment of time we may perhaps have embraced a particular profession, we may have married or been divorced, we may have formed a friendship or done wrong to a person— and now all this has become a part of our lot, our destiny. We would perhaps do things differently if we were able to return to the same situation. But "what is past never returns." We must go on, as Anouilh says, dragging the "luggage of the past" with us.

The line of time of which we spoke is like a long corridor with many doors. Year after year we open a new one. But on its other side there is no latch or knob. We cannot go back and begin anew, as the hand on the clock does. And one day—we know not when or where—the corridor will come to an end— irrevocably. The circular line on the dial of our clock, however, never comes to an end. That's why it lulls us in the illusion that it will always keep on going. The ancient hour glasses with their running sands were more honest in this respect!

So on New Year's Eve we sense this about time, we sense that every moment of our life is unique and unrepeatable, that it will never return again, and that our time runs on and one day will run out. We sense that we are finite. Moreover, we always carry this knowledge of the end around with us, even when we are not conscious of it. Without being aware of it we are constantly thinking of death. I say, for example, without thinking much about it, "I must hurry," or "I have no time." And yet when I say this I am saying that I shall not live endlessly, that I must therefore divide the limited time I have. I can only make the best of it, but I can never prolong it. "That we shall die, we know; 'tis but the time and drawing days out, that men stand upon," says Shakespeare.

The person who begins to grasp all this experiences something of a shock. Some may perhaps consider me a Beckmesser* if in all seriousness I raise the question whether many noisy New Year's Eve sprees, with their alcoholic dulling of the consciousness, may not have their origin in our desire to drown out this sound of time which suddenly grows louder at the turn of the year, and our effort to get these signs of our finitude out of our sight. In other words, there is a kind of joking that covers up and represses a deeper anxiety or an unsolved problem in our life. Every one of you has had the experience of being depressed or even in despair and saying to yourself, "Well, there's only one thing for it, cost what it may, I'll have to find something to make me laugh." And you went to a movie which you were told was really sidesplitting. And you really did laugh at some of the comical situations. But, lurking in the background, never entirely forgotten, the sadness and the unsolved problem remained. And hardly had the lights gone on again when they came back, quite unchanged.

Real joy comes only when I am in harmony with myself and with the meaning of my life from the inside out. For only when

*The pedantic town clerk in Wagner's opera, *Die Meistersinger von Nürnberg.* (Trans.)

that is so, will I escape the need to repress things by force.

So I understand very well the people who go to a service of worship on New Year's Eve, who want to hear a Word that comes from eternity, who are impelled to pray. It would be stupid to think that these people are pessimists who are always crying the blues, whereas the people with the popguns and noise-makers and the champagne corks are the optimists who affirm life. The people whom New Year's Eve drives to reflection are seeking joy too, except that they seek it in another direction. They know that our mortality, our finitude ceases to be a source of anxiety when we are safe in the hands of the Lord of time, when we are at peace with him. All that lies behind me, all the wrong I have done can no longer separate me from him. He sets it all straight. What lies ahead of me—the three hundred and sixty-five days to come—I accept from his hand. And nothing can happen to me, nothing can touch me that has not first passed his inspection and proved to be for my best welfare.

And when the last milestone is reached he will be there waiting for me. Out of this harmony with the Lord of time there comes a joy that no longer depends upon repression. For us the turn of the year should be a red light that makes us stop and look and listen, and then asks us where we are going.

❧ 6 ❧

Death and Life

On one of the first pages of the Högfeld Book we find this picture: a company of happy, carousing people are floating down a stream on a swaying, lamp-lighted boat to the sound of mandolins. As they glide down the stream, beasts of prey with glowing eyes go slinking through the darkness on both shores, waiting for the moment when the company goes ashore. Their eyes glitter greedily through the darkness, but the happy, tippling singers with their lamps and mandolins are unaware of the menacing danger. At bottom almost all of us go floating along in this way, enjoying life "as long as the little lamp glows."

Is it really necessary for me to show why people hear and see nothing? We all know the lulling mandolin sound, the siren song of the false conquerors of death, who are always telling us that they have been victorious over this "last enemy." They tell us that life is nothing more than the natural rhythm of spring, summer, autumn, and winter, the rhythm of things eternally coming and passing away. And death, they say, is nothing but a caesura, a break in this rhythm of life. All this is such a natural thing that there is no need to get excited about it.

Even our New Year's Eve customs reveal a great deal of this attitude. Why is it that people have to roar and shoot and yell and sing? Is it because on this last night of the year they have to outroar, outyell, and drown out the macabre sound of the grass growing over their own graves? They have to drown out the sound of time running out because they cannot bear to hear it. Is it really only the natural rhythm of time that reminds us again and again of the end, the death, the transiency of all that is human? It is strange, isn't it, that, if this is so, we hardly ever find a doctor who dares to tell a dying patient that he is now facing nothing more than a very "natural" process? Why can't we talk about these "natural" things, why do we have to lie, if they are so natural? May there not be something quite different from what we think behind this process of death?

Some time ago I read the following account in the diary of a young flier who died in the war. He reached out to pick a bouquet of lilacs and as he parted the branches he discovered beneath the flowering bush the half-decayed body of a soldier. He drew back in horror, not because he had never seen a dead man before—he drew back because of the screaming contradiction between the dead man and the flowering bush. If he had come upon a dead and faded lilac bush, he would not have been horrified in this way. A blooming lilac bush will one day become a withered lilac bush—this is really nothing more than the operation of the rhythm of life—but that a man should be lying there in a decayed condition, this was something that simply did not fit, and that's why he winced at the sight of it. He sensed that somehow this dead comrade was in contradiction to the Creator's plan of life. He sensed that the dead man lying there was somehow a foreign body in God's flowering world. He had become aware that the death of man is an unnatural thing. And in this, that young flier was closer to the world of the New Testament and its message than the people who are always driveling about the naturalness of human death.

Summon up in your mind's eye the picture of our Lord, going up and down the land, healing the sick, laying his hand upon the troubled and sad, forgiving sins, and raising the dead. And if we look more closely at this picture of the healing and forgiving Son of God, we shall see that the New Testament sees this whole world, this world of sin and death, of suffering and tears, as being all of a piece. Here sin, guilt, suffering, sickness, and death belong together. They are only different sides of a world that has gone off the track, a world out of joint. And therefore for Jesus Christ death is not simply a natural termination of life. It is not natural, it is not the will of God that this dark enemy should come and simply rip apart the ties of friendship, of marriage, of love. It is not simply a foregone conclusion that he must come and break his way into God's created world. It was unnaturalness incarnate, it was something contrary to God's order that this young flier sensed with his boyish instinct.

This is what the Bible teaches us with uncompromising firmness: the death of man points to an ultimate disorder; it should not be, the dark boundary posts should not stand between us and the eternal life of God. And this is precisely why this whole unnatural state of affairs, this disorder in our cracked and broken world must yield when Jesus Christ comes and lays his ordering and healing hand upon his human brethren. We are all familiar with what Alfred E. Hocke, the psychiatrist, is describing in his autobiography* when he says: "Man cannot understand his death. To him the thought is intolerable that this whole world of love and friendship, this world of work and devotion should be simply wiped out, intolerable simply to fall by the wayside, while others go on, chattering as if nothing had happened. This mocks all logic," says this physician. And whenever I stand at the deathbed or the grave of a real Christian, I feel, and all of you would feel it too, that here is a person who is at peace with God, a person whose hand is in the hand of God, and still he must depart hence like "the beasts that perish" (Ps. 49:12). Must death be? Must this limit, must the abyss continue to exist, if one is in the hands of God, the hands of the living God? This is, so to speak, the pro-

*Jahresringe.

test that always rises up within us, if we have any conception of the life which man was really intended to live. And Hölderlin was right when he said, "May God pardon me, but I cannot understand death existing in his world."

We can understand the mystery of death only if we take seriously man's rebellion against God, only if we see that death is the "wages of sin."

That's why the barrier of death has been raised against us; it teaches us that we men belong on this side of the border of transiency, that we are dust, that we are under judgment. For, down underneath, every one of us wants to be God, and Nietzsche was very honestly and bluntly telling tales outside of school when he said, "If there were gods, how could I bear not to be one?" That's what man is, and that's why the cherubim with flaming sword stands before God's eternity, saying, "Thus far shall you come and no farther." That's death as judgment, as the end; and that's what the Scriptures think of it.

Then the riven Easter tomb is nothing else than the mighty break-through point at which the Prince of life drove a breach into the enemy's front. Death could not hold him in this sealed and armored grave; he burst it asunder. And the great Easter jubilation consists in the fact that now that grave can not hold us either in the prison of death.

> Could the Head
> Rise and leave his members dead?

Could dark death be stronger than the hand that holds us; could it be stronger than the bond of faithfulness the Saviour had entered into with his disciples? Would he leave us desolate? We should then be of all men most miserable. But, praise God, we are not miserable; we are the disciples and brethren of the Risen Lord; we are, as Paul Gerhardt sang, his "companions," whom he snatches from hell and death.

To be sure, one thing remains and that is that we must die, really die. Even we Christians are not exempt from death. Jesus

himself died a real death. But even so, there is one thing that
makes a decisive difference: now this death can no longer harm
us. The serpent is still there, as Luther said, but its poison fang
has been drawn. The serpent is still there and it is still terrifying.
The horizon of our life is still encircled by the scaly armor of the
serpent of death and it is terrible, as Germanic mythology so
vividly expresses it in the symbol of the Midgard serpent. But
for us Christians something has changed: this serpent that lies
entwined about our life is dead. And for him who knows this it
has lost its terrors. The biological death which we must die
has itself been robbed of its power, it is itself dead. We must
realize in utterly practical terms that this death itself is really
dead; no longer can it snatch us from the hand of God; no longer
can it tell us its lies, saying, "Let us eat and drink, for tomorrow
we die." No longer can it tell us that there is an everlasting night
of death in which there is nothing but grievous thoughts and even
blacker realities or nothing but yawning Nothingness.

Gorch Fock wrote to his wife: "If you should hear that our
cruiser was sunk and none were saved, then do not weep. The
sea in which my body sinks is nothing but the hollow of my
Saviour's hand and nothing can snatch me from it." When Gorch
Fock wrote this, he knew very well that the ocean can be a
dreadful abyss. The hands of the Bolshevists may be the hands
of sadists, but I can pass through all this as through a wall as
thin as air, for I know Him who stands beyond that wall with
outstretched arms; in his hand this devouring ocean is a mere
pool, a little pool. How else could there ever have been such a
thing as the martyrs singing as they died or the shouts of exultation the early Christians uttered as they faced the lion's mouth?
No, they were able to sing only because their eyes pierced
through the thin wall of terror and close behind it saw the One
who was there to welcome them, no, the One who walked
through it all with them, suffering himself once more to be
crucified and devoured by lions with them. And that's the one
thing we hold on to: we must die, really die, but there is One

who goes with us; whether it be to an arena, the gallows, or a hospital bed, that One is always with us.

I close with some Gospel words of Matthias Claudius, the great German consoler:

"He that will not believe in Christ must see to it how he can get along without him. As for you and me, we cannot. We need someone who will lift and hold us up when we are alive and who will lay his hand beneath our heads when we must die, and this he can do abundantly according to what is written about him, and we know of nobody whom we'd rather have do it."

❧ 7 ❦

The Supreme Love

We certainly do not believe that the image of the noble sufferer, charming our souls by his patience, can possibly be sufficient to enable us to understand Jesus' first word from the cross, "Father, forgive them; for they know not what they do." We certainly do not think that this word has anything to do with tolerance or with stoic imperturbability. It is perhaps not too difficult—in a wild mob of people who have been whipped up by the suggestion of a demagogue to pour out wild abuse upon some very earnest man or a worthy institution—to say with a certain detachment: "They know not what they do." Indeed, there may be at work here even a kind of self-complacency that says: "After all, I am an independent man who does his own thinking, not one of the common herd."

On Golgotha, however, this word is spoken by someone who is being cruelly strangled to death on a cross, who is suffering maddening pain, almost perishing from thirst, and whose execution is not being enacted with the objective detachment of modern legal ceremonial, but rather in a welter of mockery and derision from his tormentors, and all the orgies of sadism.

Here there must be some other powers at work to bring this Man to this pitch of forgiving goodness. What are these powers?

Properly speaking, Jesus had *always* practiced what he was saying in these words. Nobody ever rose up against sin and malice as he did. How he exposed and rebuked the hypocrisy of the Pharisees, how he drove out the money-mad profaners of the temple, how earnestly he reproached the publicans and adulterers for their sins! But however terribly he hated the sinful and satanic, he loved and sought with an equal intensity those who were the victims of these powers and were living their lives in dark bondage. So when he said that we should love our neighbor as ourselves, and then was the first to practice and live out this love, he did not mean that we should try to force ourselves to something like a "feeling of love." Nobody can do this anyhow, and if we do try it, the result is only an effort for effect. It is quite impossible to love at command. Therefore he must have meant something altogether different. And so he did.

When Jesus loved a guilt-laden person and helped him, he saw in him an erring child of God. He saw in him a human being whom his Father loved and grieved over because he was going wrong. He saw him as God originally designed and meant him to be, and therefore he saw through the surface layer of grime and dirt to the real man underneath. Jesus did not *identify* the person with his sin, but rather saw in this sin something alien, something that really did not belong to him, something that merely chained and mastered him and from which he would free him and bring him back to his real self. Jesus was able to love men because he loved them right through the layer of mud.

I once heard of a woman who came to her pastor and complained bitterly about her brutal and cruel husband. She frankly acknowledged that actually she could only hate him and certainly could never love him again. The pastor then counseled her to think of him, in those times of inner anguish, as he was in the days when they were first engaged, of how he wooed her, and how the best side of him came out at that time. For *that* was what he really was. And the gradual appearance of brutality and lack of understanding was something alien which had crept into him and turned him away from his real nature. To the degree that this woman was able lovingly to get past this alien thing and see the *real* person in her distorted husband, she was able to love him again and thus bring a creatively new and constructive impulse into their ruined relationship.

This is exactly what happened here in the love and forgiveness of the dying Lord. He saw straight through the alien and distorting spirit of sadism, hatred, and blindness and looked upon all these people who were raging and roaring about his cross as homeless, unhappy children of his Father in heaven. For *them* he grieved, it was *they* whom he loved.

And when Jesus utters these words that move us so deeply, "Father, forgive them; for they know not what they do," what happens then is not something like a miracle of self-control. What happens is not anything that has to do with our will power. What happens is a miracle of a new, God-given way of seeing. The person who is given this ability to see past the filthy surface, and see the children of God despite the distortion, can also love.

We Christians are promised this transformation of our way of seeing people and we are promised it in a totally new way. For now when we are faced by those who do us wrong we must say and we are privileged to say: "Jesus Christ died for this man who is cheating us, this woman who vents her unaccountable hatred upon us, this person who is defrauding us; he bought him dearly, he has surrounded him with his love." The person who accepts the cross in *this* way when he faces stormy passages with his fellow man, and accepts the gift of *this* way of seeing— in other words, the person who sees the mystery of sonship to God in the other person—that person ceases to be merely an echo of such conflicts; he stops merely reacting to them. On the contrary, *the creative impulse of love comes into his life*. The point is that one of the persons in conflict must begin to love. Then he will be in for a surprise at how much will be changed.

That's why the moment in which this word from the cross was spoken is so tremendous. Here was One capable of loving, because he *saw* his haters and his enemies in a wholly new way. And since that moment a wholly new power has entered into the world. It is available to every one of us.

❦ 8 ❧

The Cry of Dereliction

According to the oldest account, the last word spoken by the dying Jesus is more a shriek than a saying: "My God, my God, why hast thou forsaken me?" Was not this parting cry an admission of defeat? "The sun's light failed." It was as if the sun itself could no longer abide the horrible sight. The stars shrieked—and God was silent. Again we ask, was this not capitulation?

But in this death there is something that is mysterious and different. What is in this dreadful outcry of a man apparently forsaken by God? Is he perhaps crying out his misery, his despair to the human crowd gathered around his cross? Is this outcry a kind of spiritual disburdenment? No, it is something altogether different! In the first place, it is not an unpremeditated utterance, but a strictly liturgical prayer (Psalm 22:1). The Crucified prayed a psalm. He consequently took upon his lips a word of God in order to lament his Godforsakenness. Thus, despite his distress, he still remained in contact with the divine current. He reached up for a word of the eternal God and then sent it back up again.

Anybody who expresses his anguish and his dread in such a

way that he makes the Word of God itself his witness is no longer groping and wandering about in some cosmic darkness, a deserted no man's land. No, that person is praying within the church of God, he has with him the patriarchs and prophets, all of whom are also listening to that Word and sending it back to heaven in prayer.

There is still another point to be remembered. In this cry of dereliction Jesus is not addressing the people around the cross to summon them to be witnesses of his torment. Nor does he simply cry out his agony into the empty, unheeding night of Calvary. No, he is turning to and addressing someone; he is speaking to God himself about his forsakenness. And he is not rejecting him by rebelliously denouncing the divine majesty and shouting out that as far as he was concerned he was done with God. No, he cries, "*My* God, *my* God." And so he still *has* God; the forsakenness is overcome in the very crying of it and he leaves it behind him. Real Godforsakenness is a kind of apathy that no longer finds words, unaware of anyone to address, a dull indifference that goes so far in its denial of God that it cannot even bother to forswear him, dismiss him, or hate him. For how could one forswear, how could one dismiss or hate someone who does not even exist? Jesus, however, acknowledges and confesses to the Father his utter abandonment. But in the very act of confessing it to *him* he is no longer forsaken. Now someone is there to whom he can say, "Father," someone who is still his God.

So in this cry from the utmost depths and nethermost darkness there is expressed the whole mystery of the Son of God. On the one hand it says that here he tasted the bitterest woes of human life and traversed its dark valleys and deserts of misery with his human brothers, experiencing its abysmal depths as none had ever done before. Henceforth anybody who suffers must always say to himself, "This crucified Man suffered more"; and anybody who is lonely may know that this Crucified Man passed through zones of alienation from men and God such as no man had ever endured before. That is the first thing this cry expresses:

because he cried out his Godforsakenness he was utterly human; he descended to the uttermost depths of humanity; he was man visited by the most terrible suffering and death.

Nevertheless, he is the Son of God, who, as the darkness clutched at him from below, reached out for the hand of the Father by calling out to him. And so, even as he was horribly abandoned and deserted, he was nevertheless secure in those hands and lifted above all woe. He was held suspended above the abyss of nothingness, but he was held by the majesty of God himself. As he was cast down to death, so he was secretly lifted up to an invisible throne. As he cried out like a tormented creature, so he lived in eternal communion with the Father. He is man and he is God; he is cast down into death and lifted up into life.

This is what the devout were saying when they saw in the elevation of the cross and thus in the apparent triumph of death the mysterious sign of that other elevation that was made manifest on the third day. This is what the Romanesque artists, too, were saying when they placed a crown on the head of the Crucified. One must see both crown of thorns and crown of majesty, shame and glory, death and eternity, humanity and divinity together.

❧ 9 ☙

An Easter Stroll

Early one Easter afternoon my doorbell rang. A young student whom I knew only slightly stood at the door. He apologized politely for disturbing me and asked whether he might talk with me. I saw at once that something was troubling him and proposed that we take a walk outside in the fine weather. As we ambled along the stream I hardly needed to ask him what his trouble was. He let loose of his own accord.

"Recently I have been doing a lot of thinking about questions of faith," he said. "It's true that it's all connected with several experiences that were hard to take. But that's not so important. Anyhow it suddenly struck me that this is the central question of our life. If you want to go to the movies in the evening, you ask, 'What's playing today?' Suddenly I asked myself, 'What's really being played in my life? Who is the director and who is playing the chief role?' "

I: A very sensible and obvious question. Strange, isn't it, that most people ask it only about the movies and not about their own lives?

He: Yes, that's what I suddenly realized. Then last week I heard the *St. Matthew Passion.* I did not go, as you may perhaps think, for religious reasons; not for musical reasons either. What I thought was: Here is something that has to do with the life and death of one of the most important of all men. Maybe there will be something here about this question of the direction of life. You know what I mean?

I: And how! Did you get your money's worth?

He: It hit me pretty hard. And precisely because the *St. Matthew Passion* is so undogmatic.

I: What do you mean by "undogmatic"?

He: Well, what I mean is that it doesn't talk about the Resurrection as the ministers do. The great concluding chorus merely laments the passing of this unique and lofty character. The end of the whole thing is some very human tears—not the dogma of the Resurrection.

Before I could open my mouth to ask another question, he went on almost furiously: "It's just something human like that that people understand. Everybody knows the sadness we feel when we realize that even the greatest must die and even the most brilliant meteors shine only for a moment in the sky. Tell me, why are the churches so full on Good Friday, and why are so many less full on Easter? People are moved by death, because they themselves have to die that death. They can understand the Resurrection better out there in nature than in this strange dogma in which all the sadness of Good Friday is recalled—if you don't mind my saying so—in such an unseemly way."

I: You're right; your analysis would apply to the majority of people. But the only question is what conclusion we are to draw from this. What you are saying, aren't you, if I have understood you, is that everybody, from the creator of the *St. Matthew Passion* to all these nicely dressed people around us, has some feeling for the human, moving element in the Good Friday death, but not for the empty grave of Easter and other miracles?

He: That's exactly what I mean. And look here [my friend said with vehemence], it's simply a mystery to me how someone like you, who gives lectures on *Faust* and whom I recently saw at the football field, can have anything to do with the miracle of the Resurrection. That's true, isn't it—or don't you?

I: Of course it's true. If Christ did not rise from the dead, then his life and his work are refuted. From Bethlehem to Golgotha there is not a single scene in this life which is not indirectly illuminated by the light of Easter and which is not sustained by the certainty that the life of this One Man is not bounded by death, but that it is stronger than death. If I didn't know that, and if I were not also convinced that this One Man also carries his own, and therefore me too, right through the same death, then I wouldn't even dare to ask the question of what is being played out in my life.

He: I'm really glad that you say this so bluntly and unintellectually. But actually you only put me more at a loss. Does this mean that we who go for Good Friday and can't go along with Easter are not Christians? Why then is the story of the Passion in the Gospels so detailed and the Easter account so short? Why does the *St. Matthew Passion* conclude with the burial of Jesus without dealing with the mysteries of the third day? Isn't it always the human fate of the Crucified that moves us, and isn't Easter more a doctrinaire, forced, and artificial appendix? One is shot through with life and the other is a bloodless doctrine. Well, I've said it straight out. It bothers me and I can't keep quiet about it.

I: You don't have to keep quiet about it at all. After all, one can't buy faith at the price of dishonesty. First, allow me to make an altogether naïve remark. Have you ever read the Easter accounts when somebody who was very near to you died—your father, your mother, your friend? No? But I have. Such situations are a stern test of genuineness. Then you sense every false note. And speculations don't count at all when you are elementally wrought up. But the Easter accounts are themselves elemental. They have a freshness that banishes the gloom of the grave. You must try it sometime. There is nothing "bloodlessly doctrinal" about them.

He: Good. That sounds like a suggestion worth listening to. Strange that you, a scientific scholar, should say that to me. It doesn't sound very scientific!

I: There are moments when the scholar must confess what he lives by himself and declare where the elements lie that move his thinking.

He: After all, as a theologian you are well versed in speculation. That's why I appreciate the fact that you have addressed me from a completely different point of view. But tell me, please, something more about this fact that Good Friday with all its humanness interests people, while Easter is a kind of addition difficult to digest—at least in their consciousness.

I: It's just the other way around from what you think. For the people of the New Testament—and for Bach, too—the Easter certainty was settled. Their faith lived on the certainty that in this One Man the mystery of God himself entered in among us. For them the most self-evident fact in the world was that what happened in Jesus of Nazareth had to do with God himself. But that he forsook the "base headquarters in heaven," that he came down into the front-line trenches where we live, that he endured sin, suffering and death with his human brothers —this was the great mystery. That's why they devoted every effort in their accounts and in their reflection to this one absurd, incredible fact, that he really and truly lived and suffered as a man, as one of us.

Don't you see? We say today: Good Friday is so human and therefore so credible, but Easter is a legend. But the great Christians throughout the centuries have thought just the opposite: Easter is clear. Death is a miserable weakling compared with the Son of God. But that this Son of God should have been a man like us—this may perhaps be a legend, this may perhaps be only a story. It was from this point of view then that they fought and debated about the man Jesus and the human element in Good Friday.

He: Then this would mean that then people fought about Good Friday and that we today must contend about Easter?

I: That's it precisely!

He: Just a moment! What did you say? Excuse me, I'll have to digest that first.

❧ 10 ❧

Living by the Resurrection

There is nothing in life so certain as the fact that we must die. If the Easter message is to help us to come to terms with death, then it must be at least as certain as that fact. But isn't it simply grotesque to accept that this strange report of an ancient story—that the grave of Jesus of Nazareth was empty on the third day and that therefore *we* too will rise from death and decay—has any effect upon the elementary fact of our biological end? What the Psalm says about man being "like the beasts that perish" may sound somewhat drastic; nevertheless it is right, and our experience confirms it. But that Christ carries us through the night of the grave into eternal life—what experience could ever prove such a thing? Would we seriously doubt the certainty of the Pythagorean proposition if somebody told us about a dream he had had in which he had experienced a totally different kind of geometry? Can one (this would, after all, be a parallel question) doubt the certainty and finality of one's own death just because we read in an old chronicle that a few people in an ancient land had a vision that their spiritual leader had come alive again?

To be quite honest about it, we must admit that it is intolerable for all of us, including us Christians, that our temporal and eternal destiny should be dependent upon such a relative, such a rickety thing as a millenniums-old chronicle and the approval or disapproval of the historians. An absolute such as faith in the Easter victory over death dare not hang by the thin threads of such doubtful relativities.

But the Easter story teaches us that this is not the case. It is interesting to see how Jesus Christ himself deals with the question of resurrection in the parable of the rich man and Lazarus.

In the parable the rich man sits in the hell of eternal separation from God and thinks about his five flippant brothers who are still walking unsuspecting in the light. He considers how one might administer a salutary shock to them to keep them from heading toward the abyss. He hits upon the idea of asking Abraham to send a messenger from the world beyond to give them a clear warning by giving them a first-hand account of heaven and hell, eternal life and eternal death.

Abraham flatly refuses, however, and makes it clear to the rich man that his brothers have "Moses and the prophets" and that they can learn everything that is necessary from the Word of God without any such spectacular appearance from the world beyond. If they wished to cut themselves off from this Word, then no impression would be made upon them if someone came from the realm of the dead and treated them to eyewitness accounts. What Abraham means is that if anyone is not inwardly touched by the reality which is in question here and if he does not want to be disturbed in "the prime flush of his sins" by any interjections from the beyond, he will surely find reasons enough to argue away such miracles. Then he will perhaps speak of them as spiritualistic delusions.

One could say exactly the same of the disciples on Easter morning: the disciples could never have been persuaded to believe that the dead Jesus had risen from the grave if they had not believed his *Word*. They would have had plenty of other explanations, such as the familiar one that the body of Jesus had been stolen or transported somewhere else by a few of his followers with the studied purpose of building up a legend. A miracle never yet brought anyone to faith. It can always be explained in some other way. (This is why Jesus refused the challenges to legitimate himself by performing miracles.) So even the empty grave did not bring the disciples to faith. Something quite different happened: in view of the empty grave the scales suddenly fell from their eyes and afterward they realized how many dotted lines in the life of the Saviour pointed to and intersected at this one point where the event of Easter burst upon them. What they experienced on that morning was only the final total of a sum of events, of which, it is true, they had been eyewitnesses, but which they had not really understood at all in the moment when they happened.

Then, after the event, it really dawned on them that when someone says, "Your sins are forgiven," and the person addressed *actually* stands up and walks away a new man, then the only person who could say this must be one who was himself *not* involved in the fatal guilt of all mankind, but was mysteriously beyond it. When someone says, "Young man, I say to you, arise," and the dead man actually rises up and is returned to his grieving mother, then this could only happen if this were a person from whom death, the "last evening," has been forced to retreat. Further, the words "come to me, all who labor and are heavy-laden," could only be spoken by someone who himself understood all the weariness and torment and shared it like a brother, but whose life was nevertheless fed by other springs and from whose body flow streams of living water.

All this, which the disciples most assuredly experienced, but which, because their eyes were strangely "holden," they had not yet taken in, suddenly dawned upon them in the light of Easter. The whole life of the wandering Saviour, who had gone through the land healing, helping, forgiving, and bestowing new beginnings, suddenly became transparent to them. It was as if hitherto they had seen the colored windows in the sanctuary of this unique life only from the outside. The panes were dark and the language of the pictures was obscure. But when these people were transported to the interior of this mystery on Easter morning, the pictures sprang into life and took on sight and speech. That which had seemed gray to them before, the mute, empty meaninglessness of which had plunged them into the panic of Golgotha and caused them to doubt everything, now became for them an eloquent and compelling sign. Suddenly they realized that while he was on earth and they shared his daily life, they had not really known him at all. True, their hearts had burned within them and they dimly felt that they were walking in the shadow of a mighty figure; but not till now did they discover *who* it was that walked with them there. Afterward the light came into his enigmatic words and acts and the heavens opened above the one they thought was only one of themselves, even though the greatest among men—now he turned out to be the "totally Other," who came from the eternity of the Father and shared for a little while their life on earth.

That's why the Easter fact will never convince us, if the Man does not convince us. It's not the empty grave that wins us to faith, nor can any Resurrection account do this. Only this risen Man can do it. When we meet Jesus of Nazareth we realize that here is someone who for love's sake united his lot with our human lot and keeps faith with us. This is the only reason why the chorale, "When I depart, depart thou not from me," can have a place in the *St. Matthew Passion.* The person who is gripped by this solidarity with Jesus Christ knows that he does not allow death to come between him and me, but that I am safe with him for all eternity. And here perhaps our experience may be the same as that of the disciples. It may dawn upon us only afterward. Perhaps at first we gather only that here was a man who walked the earth and loved with an absolute love, with no regard for what it cost. This is true, of course, but it is still not the ultimate thing. For then we should have touched only the hem of his garment, but not yet seen his face. And yet it would be a beginning. I have no use for the crass alternative that one must either believe everything at once or remain an unbeliever. Faith, too, is a matter of growth, of small beginnings and ultimate fulfillments. But one

thing is sure: if we begin to read the Gospels very simply as interesting stories about all kinds of human beings (and why shouldn't
we?), the day will come when we shall see that this comparison
no longer applies and that there are totally different realities behind
it all. Only then will we have arrived at the real thing. Then the
colored windows will begin to shine and the Prince of life will
look straight at us and say: "You shall not die, but live."

❧ 11 ❧

The Miracle of the Spirit

Sometimes in our younger days when we stayed overnight in a youth hostel or camp, our excess energy exploded into all kinds of mischief. We descended upon innocent sleepers or dressed up as ghosts and had all kinds of fun when a small panic broke out in the dark room. We used to call this game "Here comes the Holy Ghost." This may still be the name for it today. But why exactly should it be called by *this* name?

Undoubtedly what we meant to say was: "Tonight we are playing a really silly game." And in our conception the Holy Ghost doubtless had some connection with craziness. Anybody who had anything to do with the Holy Ghost must be crazy.

This is what the spectators at the Pentecost event meant, too, as you may read in the Book of Acts (go ahead and read it; it's in the second chapter). They declared that the disciples, upon whom the Spirit had come, had actually been drinking too much. As far as they were concerned, that's all there was to it; one could see that without subjecting them to a blood test.

But this supposition simply did not add up. For somehow these people were willing to be put in prison for what they were supposed to have seen in delirium; they were willing to be stoned and bullied for it. This should have given the spectators pause, for alcoholic visions usually give way to a hangover. In any case, nobody is going to give up his life for such a vision. Generally one gives up one's life only for something which one has determined in a state of realistic soberness to be a matter of extreme importance, a matter, therefore, for which even in the closest calculation the price of life itself is not too high. Anybody who reads these stories of what happened at Pentecost will find that these were people who calculated and argued in utter soberness. And even the accounts themselves are as spare and matter-of-fact as police records.

But then what is meant by this strange term "Holy Ghost"?

What the disciples were saying was: "Suddenly the scales have fallen from our eyes. We knew before that Christ was crucified and rose again. But we could do nothing with it. To us it was like Chinese music. Now, all of a sudden, we know what it means; now it *speaks* to us. Now it concerns us so much that we must change our lives."

This can be made plain by an example. Surely you have seen an ancient cathedral with windows of stained glass. Often these windows depict stories of the Bible—Adam and Eve, the prophets, Mary beneath the cross of her Son, the women at the grave of the Saviour. But if you go round the church on the outside, you will not see this at all. The windows seem to be dull and drab. But if you go inside, they shine in all the richness of their color. In a way they preach the old stories. And anyone who takes the time can spend a whole hour listening to the pictures speaking. On the outside, however, they do not speak. They do not concern us at all.

Pentecost is an event through which we are, as it were, set down within the church where the pictures and stories begin to speak. Perhaps everything you learned in Sunday school and confirmation instruction looks dull and gray to you and says nothing to you. Then definitely that is a sign that you are seeing the windows from the wrong side and that the miracle of the Spirit has not yet led you to the inside. You and the disciples are looking at the same windows, but each is seeing them from the other side.

This happens elsewhere in life too. If you look at a mother's love from the outside, as a cold, merely biological observer, then it, too, looks rather colorless—that is to say, like some kind of foolish fondness induced by glandular secretions. But when you think of your own mother, the peace of her protection, the warmth of her heart, her loving thoughts, then the picture of a mother suddenly bursts into bloom in full and warm color. Then you see mother love from the inside, as does a child that belongs to its mother.

So it is with the Holy Spirit. As he leads us into the interior of the house of God where the windows shine, suddenly we are no longer mere spectators and onlookers. Suddenly it becomes clear to us that the Father knows *us*, that we are his children. Once we are inside we see that it was not just anybody who once was hanged upon the cross, but that he died for *me*. There I am suddenly drawn into the events of the pictures; all at once I become an actor and I, too, find myself standing with the rest beneath the cross and at the open grave. Suddenly *my* sins are forgiven and I can begin life anew.

That's what the disciples meant when they said: "The scales have suddenly fallen from our eyes." Suddenly they knew: *I* am the one who is meant; God has looked at me and my life, and now I can no longer evade that gaze. Now I am being confronted with the question: Are you going in or are you going to go on strike and keep on in the same old rut?

❧ 12 ❧

The Parable of the Treasure in the Field and the Pearl of Great Price

The kingdom of heaven is like treasure hidden in a field, which a man found and covered up; then in his joy he goes and sells all that he has and buys that field.

Again, the kingdom of heaven is like a merchant in search of fine pearls, who, on finding one pearl of great value, went and sold all that he had and bought it.

MATTHEW 13:44-46

We cannot say that the people in the Bible were all made on the same last. We cannot say that the Bible always deals with the same type of people, namely, people who have had unusual religious experiences or possess a kind of piety which we look upon partly with estrangement and partly with admiration, people with some special kind of religious antennae which we modern people feel we do not possess. On the contrary, the people of the Bible present such a profusion of types, temperaments, and characters that the impression we get is as many-colored as life itself.

What a great contrast there is, for example, between the somewhat impetuous Peter, who was so bold to believe, and the self-tormenting skeptic, Thomas, and Judas who rebelled against everything and failed so dreadfully! And so it is everywhere in the Bible, wherever we may meet them. On the one hand there is the rich young ruler who sought and sought for the meaning of his life and then at the critical moment failed to find it after all. And there on the other hand is the farmer who wasn't looking for anything at all, but simply doing his daily routine work, and yet, contrary to all expectation, found "everything."

Somewhere in this rich and variegated play and interplay of types, characters, and destinies, you and I, too, are represented. And so we ask what there is of this farmer and this merchant that is in us.

How did the farmer find the kingdom of God?

The first thing we note is that the kingdom of God is hidden; God isn't knocking about the streets. Fundamentally, this is always the greatest offense, that God should make so little fuss about himself, that he hardly makes any external appearance at all, and even when he does it is ambiguous, that one cannot even say what can be said of any tree or any automobile, "See, there it is!" A pound of beef makes a good soup. That's sure as shooting. But what is sure as shooting about God?

Or is not this business of God being present to us only in the venture of faith, his remaining in the realm of the undemonstrable an all too airy affair; is not this merely an appeal to credulity? A bowl of beef soup and God! Well, even a trivial thing can often land us in the heart of a problem. And this applies also to this old refrain of the atheists.

Once there was one who wanted to get Christ out on the streets where everybody could see him. He wanted to provide him with flags and emblems of sovereignty; he wanted to give him publicity. But the one who wanted to do this was the devil; and, to be sure, his proposal that Christ should go out into the streets and let himself be seen in the streets was extremely tempting. The disciples would have exulted, for some of the splendor of this visible, indubitable glory would have fallen upon them. Nobody would have dared to despise them if they were cabinet ministers of so great a Lord, the honored burgesses of a theocracy. Nor would John have needed to send an embassy from prison to inquire whether this Jesus was really the one he was waiting for, the one in whom the world's destiny would be fulfilled. He would not have needed to doubt—*if* Christ had gone out into the streets.

But look, he chose another way. He came into the world through its most hidden door. He was born a poor child in a little hole-and-corner town on the edge of the world. He comforted the weeping, blessed the children, and laid his hand upon the despairing. But these poor, sick, miserable people are not to be found on the avenue of triumph where kings come marching in. They shuffle and crouch in the dark and hidden corners, they live in the attics and barracks of the poor, and sometimes, of course, in the loneliness of an executive's office.

Why did he choose this way, instead of seizing the power and publicity which were available to him? Jesus did *not* want people to be overwhelmed by the marching steps of the twelve legions of angels he could have summoned as he hung upon the cross, and which he did *not* summon. Perhaps, as we think back on the past millenium, he never wanted anything like a Christian culture and Christian states in which everybody was automatically dumped into the big sack of Christendom and included as a matter of course among the possessors of baptismal certificates simply by being born and by the operation of ecclesiastical custom, even though they had no personal relationship whatsoever to Jesus of Nazareth. And perhaps we owe it to the goodness of God that all this crumbled away in our hands and continues to do so.

In any case, Jesus did not wish all of this. He wants no wholesale Christianity in the mass; he has no desire for the church's propaganda orgies. What he wants is quite simply and quietly to meet and gaze at each one of us individually. And as we stand there in utter stillness and solitude, before him who is, as it were, illuminated from within by the fullness of God that dwells in him, we suddenly become aware that we have lost God, that we are homeless, and that a great gulf yawns between us and our

Father. And as this becomes clear to us, standing there before this quiet Figure, we note at the same time that *he* is standing in the midst of the gulf, helping us to get across, that his cross is like a bridge flung across the abyss. We see that he is suffering and dying and bearing the sin with us, that in everything he is one of us, our comrade in the abyss and in death.

Could he have done all this as a king at the head of twelve legions of angels? Could he have done this if he had come striding down the parade ground clothed in purple robes, if he had been prominent, a star, if behind him was to be heard the throbbing rhythm of his marching columns?

No—this he could do only if he stooped so low that every one of us is compelled to say: "I am poor, but this my Brother is still poorer; I face the agony of death, but this my Brother tasted it to the dregs; I feel that I am forsaken of God, but this my Brother endured the bitterness of that separation to that last extremity in the darkness of Golgotha where he cried out more pitifully than I have ever needed to do even in my darkest hours."

That's why Jesus did not go striding through the world as a messianic king with twelve legions of angels. Then every one of us could have seen and saluted him only from afar, across the cold distance with which the great of this world are accustomed to cordon themselves off from the rest of us. That's why he was the poor carpenter's son like thousands of others. That's why he died like all his human brothers. That's why he spared himself nothing that others too must bear. There is something pitiable in every one of us, even though outwardly we may cut a quite passable figure. In one way or another we are all standing "alone in the rain." And it is precisely at *this* level of the self, where we are poor and alone, that Jesus is our Brother.

And that's why—and this is the other corollary—he became the hidden, secret King, so hidden that one can easily overlook him, so hidden that one can walk the fields of Nazareth, Bethlehem, and Golgotha without ever seeing him, that one can even enter the field of the church without seeing the pearl in all the muck and all the petty trappings. It pleased God not to mount the pearl of sonship to God in a golden setting and place it in the gala show window of one of our great cities, where it cannot be reached and only the wise, the wealthy, and the plutocrats of this world can buy it. No, it pleased him rather to put it in a very ordinary field, a field like any other field, where the heavy and toilsome steps of men are trod, and where even the poorest can find it.

So there is one thing at any rate that we can learn in this hour, and that is that we shall not be like those blasé people who ask, "Can anything good come out of Nazareth?" and be offended by the poor and stony field in which the pearl lies hidden. We shall not be offended by the fact that this pearl—Jesus Christ—lay in the field of a country situated on the periphery of world events and which is in many respects alien to us. We shall not allow this to reduce it to merely relative importance. We shall not be offended by the fact that it appeared in an age to which we of the age of atomic power and jet planes imagine we are superior.

Rather we shall love the pearl because it did not think itself too good to be buried in that poor field and because therefore it does not think itself too good to be picked up today by our poor and empty hands. In these hands—and what have not these hands done!—in these hands we can take and press to our hearts the very glory of God. In these mouths of ours—and what villainies and devastations have not poured out from them!—we may receive his gift of grace at the table of the Lord. If the field was not too sordid for him, so shall our hands be not too soiled for him, either.

So it is because of love and profound condescension that God is hidden in the field. We must search for him as one seeks the figure in a picture puzzle.

Now, what is this field? The field in which the treasure lies is nothing else but the territory upon which our life is enacted. The field is our life in which we do our work or simply loaf along.

And in this our life the hiddennes of God is just like that treasure in the field. How many a pearl is hidden in a pain that comes into our life; in the affliction, that we must endure when we stand at the grave of a loved one, when homesickness consumes us in year after year of captivity, when our marriage breaks down, or when men are unjust to us.

The laborer in the field was probably dismayed at first when his plow struck an obstacle. His first outburst may have been, "Oh, these confounded stones!" How often we fume and fret over the hard lumps of fate which the plow of our life strikes, the senseless blocks that fate flings in our way. Whereas in reality it is the pearl, the treasure, which is waiting to be found.

Perhaps there is someone among us who has come here after a decade of captivity to pay to God the debt of his gratitude. He may still be struggling to throw off the net that these terrible years have thrown around him. The desolation of the hopelessness he endured, the sadism perpetrated upon him by men, these still keep reaching out their tentacles and prevent him from feeling at home. He is still a restless wanderer in the no man's land between two worlds, between the dark, horrible world that lies behind him and his homeland, which to him is still as strange and incomprehensible as was Ithaca to Odysseus when he awoke one morning on its shore.

And yet, when he looks back, must not even he (the man whose miseries keep pursuing him in his dreams) confess that even in the midst of the ghastly gray or the blood red of those demonic years this mysterious pearl shed forth its gleam time and time again? Did he not experience consolations of which people who live in respectable security know nothing at all? Did not there come to him here and there a good word that shone and gleamed as light can only in extreme darkness? Was he not directed and guided to the way out that looks upward and to the consolations from above with an intensity that seldom occurs on the smooth asphalt streets of "normal life"? And do not those words, "Now thank we all our God," that were sung at his homecoming, ring in his ears with a note that we perhaps can never hear when we sing them in church? Has anyone—apart from the angels—ever heard such singing; has anyone ever seen the shining eyes of the children with their bouquets of flowers—perhaps the eyes of his own children—in such a way as he? And does not the shining light of this unutterable homecoming have its real source in the splendor of that pearl which lies in the darkest fields?

Is not all of this, the hardships and the shining moments, one clear unconquerable call to see the hidden mercies of God in all the strange and puzzling things that happen to us, and to trust the higher thoughts which God is thinking about our life?

In short, the pearl is concealed in pain; it is hidden like a treasure in the broken, furrowed field.

But there is still something more that our parable shows us. The man makes a sacrifice and sells everything he has in order to acquire the treasure.

To understand the prodigiousness of what happened we must try to imagine the consternation on the faces of his neighbors and friends when he plunged into this utterly incomprehensible expense to buy a field whose value appeared to have no relation at all to the financial sacrifice he was making. The people actually thought, The man is crazy! He sold literally all that he had, even the things that were elementary necessities, in order to buy this field. He did what the rich young ruler did not do.

And here the text touches a tender point about which we, as those who are or want to become Christians, must make up our minds. For this is what it says: "God is never thrown at you for free; he always costs something." Perhaps the loving indulgence with which Jesus sought out the lost, so that no dive, no publican's home was too mean for him to visit, may have misled some of us into the error of thinking that Jesus throws himself at people even against their will. If this were so, well, then there's still plenty of time to settle the question of eternity. Then whenever we come will be early enough.

No, God isn't simply thrust upon us for nothing. Everything in the world must be paid for—even God. And when we declare and confess that God does not act in terms of work-righteousness, but that everything comes to us through unspeakable grace, this does not mean that the grace of God has anything to do with larks falling ready roasted into our mouths. What it has to do with is precisely this pearl, this treasure which must be purchased with all that we have.

I believe that in this respect, too, the time of trial which lies behind us and which our brethren in the East are still going through has served to clarify the meaning of faith. For faith is certainly no longer a matter of roasted larks. Christian faith has begun to cost something. Don't begin to feel too confident and secure in this bit of calm weather we still have here in West Germany! Plans have already been made (one needs only to read Robert Jungk's book, *The Future Has Already Begun*, to be assured of this) to see to it that one day the puppets will begin to dance in the West too. And nobody can guarantee the church of Jesus Christ—nor does God do so—that it, that you and I will not once more be confronted in actuality with the harsh *either-or* of Luther's hymn: *either* "goods, fame, child, and wife," *or* "the kingdom that must remain to us."

And even if this should not come to pass, we must still ask ourselves whether there are not many things in our life that are more cherished and more important to us than Jesus Christ, and whether these more important things may not one day become the price for which we sell our Christian faith: a passion, a particular style of living, an infidelity, a business manipulation— or whatever form the masks of the Wicked One may take.

"Let anyone who thinks that he stands take heed lest he fall." In any case, I myself have seen veritable oaks of faith fall, trees whose roots in God's earth simply could not contend, at the critical moment, with the winds of the times that assailed their crowns and ripped them from the ground. Who knows whether and when we shall not all have to choose between our roots and those winds?

And there they are again, those troublesome, tiresome words which have been hanging over the Christian life from the beginning and which have made many feel that it was a hot iron that had better not be touched, the words: *either-or*. Sell this and leave that! The words, "You cannot serve God and mammon."

Does not our Christian life always have in it something of this negative note of renunciation? So it was with the man in the parable. He had to give up almost everything that filled his life in order to gain the treasure.

But now one need only look at his face to judge how he feels. It says that he went "in his joy" to get rid of all that he had. He is not pulling a long face, contorted with pain, and saying to himself, "Well, I have recognized God's earnest demands and now for good or evil I must draw the consequences." No, "in his joy he goes and sells all that he has." For, after all, what was his great discovery? Now he could say: "This treasure, this pearl outweighs everything, everything! It outshines all the losses, all the mockery of my neighbors, all the clinging to cherished habits and cherished things. It compensates me a hundredfold for all the material losses and all the restrictions upon my standard of living which I must accept in order to have this one, great thing of my life."

This is the message of this text. Certainly the Christian faith often presents us with conflicts at points where the people of the world have no inhibitions whatsoever. Often it confronts us with an *either-or* that creates hardship and in moments of weakness makes us look somewhat enviously at the careless nonchalance of the indifferent.

But what we must see is that the emphasis is *not* upon what we give up but what we receive. That's why the Christians walked into the jaws of lions, not with clenched teeth, but with praises on their lips. That's why the disciples sang as they climbed the scaffold. That's why it is not somber asceticism, but a soaring, swinging, sustaining thought that makes us sing:

> Grant, O God, that I may care,
> In life and death, for naught,
> But find the one thing needful
> In that which Christ has wrought.

The light of this pearl gleams in the darkness of the catacombs and shines in the gloom of every pain that anyone ever has or ever will suffer for Jesus' sake. And those who have so suffered have testified that the deeper the darkness grew in their bomb

shelters, their prison cells, and their sickrooms, the more brightly
did the pearl begin to shine. So Christians are by nature happy
people, and when they lose their sense of humor it is nothing
less than a denial of their Lord.

Then there is still another point we must consider. When the
man had found the treasure, for him everything was changed. He
saw the world with completely new and different eyes. That's
the way it always is; when we have found something altogether
precious—a life partner, a friend, or a fulfillment in our life's
work—then everything else gets measured by it and slips into
second place; it is given its relative value. How differently the man
looked at the field now! No longer did he gauge the field by its
actual value or its productiveness, but by the fact that the
treasure was in it. To ordinary eyes it looked like all other fields.
But the farmer knew the secret that lay hidden in its soil.

So as we Christians follow Jesus we receive not only a new
heart, but also new eyes. We see the pearl in things. And this
applies to all kinds of things. How different nature becomes,
how different a sunrise, how different the autumn fruits of the
field, when we have discovered the pearl and the treasure! Then
we can no longer look upon all this merely aesthetically, enjoy
it merely as a piece of earthly beauty. Now we see it with the
eyes of Psalm 104 as one great jubilant hymn of praise to the
Creator, and through the "clouds and winds and waters" we look
straight into the heart of the Father who allows us to be his
beloved children in the midst of this garden of his glory and
makes the eyes of all to wait upon him. Suddenly we see nature
with different eyes—just as the farmer looked at the field with
quite different eyes after he had found the treasure.

And suddenly how different our neighbor looks! Now he is
no longer—at least not primarily—the man who uses us or hurts
us, the man we like or do not like. Suddenly he becomes in
our eyes the bearer of the precious pearl. Even though he may
be a poor or wicked wretch, a stony, unproductive field with
which not much can be done, we see now that he has been dearly
purchased, that the eye of our Saviour is upon him and that he

gave himself for him to win him for eternity. Suddenly our transformed eyes see, as Luther put it, that he wears a golden chain about his neck, that he is the bearer of a hidden treasure. There is nothing that Jesus does not transform when he steps into our life. He pervades everything and plows up our whole life, and we ourselves become people with new eyes when Jesus looks at us. And where others, where the farmer's neighbors, see only a stony field, we descry the precious secret of God.

Do we understand now why the farmer sold everything and left all, gave everything away for sheer joy and exultation? For now it was clear as day to him: One thing is needful, and that's this treasure. If I have that, then I'll have everything else too. But first I must have the treasure.

We all make the mistake of not letting God be the one and only thing, of making him only a religious addition to life but not life itself. A "bit" of God, a "bit" of religion in the midst of the gray of everyday life and the harshness of competition— who would want to get along without it! It gives a little light to the daily misery, provides a bit of cushioning, and blunts the sharpness of the day's toil. A "bit" of God!

But God is no such addition, and the pearl is not an ornament to delight us in weary moments. If the man had not put everything else beneath the pearl, if he had not sold all that he had and laid it all on the line, he would never have gained it, but seen it only from afar, and its splendor would have passed him by. But even more, he would have grown unhappy, because he would never be able to forget the pearl.

How many people there are who actually are thrown into this kind of conflict through Jesus Christ, people who are made unhappy because of him! Down in their hearts they say to themselves, "This I must have. He could make my life rich and new." But at the same time they love the other thing, the thing they will not leave: the career which must not be disturbed, the respect of men which they will not expose to derision, their money, their comfort and convenience which must not be put at the disposal of a neighbor's need. And because they will not leave all these things, because they want to carry water on both shoulders—the water of God and the water of mammon—they never gain the pearl and their hearts are ground and rasped in discord, which often enough spills over into open hatred of the troublemaker, Jesus Christ. "The half-hearted gain neither freedom nor the kingdom of heaven." It is not Jesus Christ who makes us restless and divided, but our divided hearts, which would do this one thing, but will not leave off doing all the other things.

So when Jesus says, "One thing is needful," this is a call to struggle, a summons to battle against all the multiplicity of things that still possess and hold us captive.

But at the same time it is a call to freedom.

When we have this one thing, we acquire the quiet eyes and the long view of those who no longer lose themselves in the fears and cares and hopes of all that runs across our daily path, but know what abides in the end when everything else fails; those who gain a standard for what is great and small in the kingdom of God and therefore recoil from many things in which the world carelessly concurs; and conversely, those who learn to sing and praise and laugh where the world loses its nerve.

Have our eyes been made new? How different the fields and the world look, now that we may be stewards of the mysteries of God! How small and cheap so many things look now, which before seemed so great and desirable; and how attractive and happy so many things, which before we despised! This is the transvaluation of all values wrought by the discipleship of Jesus.

❧ 13 ❧

The Parable of the Unmerciful Servant

Then Peter came up and said to him, "Lord, how often shall my brother sin again me, and I forgive him? As many as seven times?" Jesus said to him, "I do not say to you seven times, but seventy times seven.

"Therefore the kingdom of heaven may be compared to a king who wished to settle accounts with his servants. When he began the reckoning, one was brought to him who owed him ten thousand talents; and as he could not pay, his lord ordered him to be sold, with his wife and children and all that he had, and payment to be made. So the servant fell on his knees, imploring him, 'Lord, have patience with me, and I will pay you everything.' And out of pity for him the lord of that servant released him and forgave him the debt. But that same servant, as he went out, came upon one of his fellow servants who owed him a hundred denarii; and seizing him by the throat he said, 'Pay what you owe.' So his fellow servant fell down and besought him, 'Have patience with me, and I will pay you.' He refused and went and put him in prison till he should pay the debt. When his fellow servants saw what had taken place, they were greatly distressed, and they went and reported to their lord all that had taken place. Then his lord summoned him and said to him, 'You wicked servant! I forgave you all that debt because you besought me; and should not you have had mercy on your fellow servant, as I had mercy on you?' And in anger his lord delivered him to the jailers, till he should pay all his debt. So also my heavenly Father will do to every one of you, if you do not forgive your brother from your heart."

MATTHEW 18:21-35

We cannot determine with any certainty what it was that prompted Peter to ask this remarkable question: "How often shall my brother sin against me, and I forgive him?" Two different motives suggest themselves.

First, Peter may have had something like this in mind: This Jesus of Nazareth whom I am following is certainly not hard on anybody. Though one of us may have the secret thought that after all it is a shocking thing even to allow oneself to be seen with a common woman, a functionary of the occupying power, or a publican, this not only makes no difference to him but he even approaches these people and other trash like them with a friendliness and indulgence which may at first be impressive but will soon get on your nerves. After all, if he is going to be so utterly limitless in his forbearance, this puts a kind of moral demand upon everybody around him. And what this demand implies is this: I expect that you too will not return hatred for hatred, that you too must not allow yourself to be touched by secret pharisaism when you meet a guilt-laden person who has come down in the world.

Peter may have thought: It is simply too much of a hardship to be constantly subject to this demand and never be able to burst out and really let yourself go. Surely there must be some place where we must call a halt to this everlasting indulgence and kindness. After all, a man must have an opportunity at some point to blow up and speak his mind.

But it is possible that Peter had something quite different in mind when he asked his question. He may have said to himself: "If I make an offer to forgive seven times, this is, after all, a pretty good quantity of kindness. This really should please him no end. He will probably even disagree with me and say: 'Don't go too far with this forgiving, Peter. You can't be too squashy

soft with your debtors either. Otherwise the time will come when
they won't take their debts seriously. Seven times is really too
much. Don't be too zealous a Christian, Peter! It's not good
policy.' "

But whatever the motive that prompted Peter to ask his question, one thing is certain: he is trying to get Jesus to sanction a
limitation upon Christian love of one's neighbor. For, as you
know, it is in many ways very reassuring to know when and
where one can *stop* loving one's neighbor with good conscience.
Generally, to know the answer to this question is of more interest
and importance to us than the question of when and where we
must *begin* to love our neighbor.

In the first place, it makes us feel more comfortable morally
to be able to say: "Here I have really fulfilled my quota of love
and forbearance. No more is required of me, even God doesn't
ask for more." It is the charm of all religions of law that they
assign to a person a definite and limited quantum of obligations,
of work, sacrifice, love, and decorum. And when a man has fulfilled his quota he is, so to speak, pensioned off and he can relax
with a good conscience.

In the second place, we are interested in this limitation upon
love because our flesh is constantly posing the question: "When
can I really let go? When do I have a right to explode?" When I
was a student of theology I once had a real termagant for a land-
lady who gave me plenty of opportunity to exercise my Christian love and patience. The situation finally became too much for
me and I discussed with an older friend of mine how I might give
this dragon a proper knock. He said, "As a future pastor you
really cannot do that." And my reply was, "But after all, I too
am only a human being; this is the limit and I'm through."

The limit! This is what Peter was asking about. He wanted
to know when it is reached. For Peter, as we know, had a
temper, and he was afraid that never again would he be allowed
to let go and vent his anger. He too must have thought, "After
all, I'm only a human being." As a rule, when we say something
like this we mean: "After all, I too am the kind of person who

74 *Christ and the Meaning of Life*

reacts to what others do to me. Ultimately, I am only an echo of
my environment, and I just can't swallow everything that is done
to me."

And this brings us right to the theme of the parable. For here
the Lord shows us two things. First, that we are *not* the echo of
our environment but rather the echo of what God has done for
us. Secondly, he shows us that we are human beings, not because we can permit ourselves to explode, but because we can
exhibit and pass on to others what God has given to us.

The chief culprit in our parable is a man who stands between
his king and his neighbor. He therefore stands in a double relationship. If we were to ask the question: What is man? it would
be utterly absurd to answer it by pointing to what one sees and
observes in man. In this case one would have to say—and note that
this has been said, I myself read it in a book!—"Man is a feather-
less biped." But if we say this "we lump him together with a
plucked rooster, a kangaroo, or a jerboa." And this in itself shows
that when we describe only the external aspect of man we have
failed to grasp what is distinctive in man, what distinguishes him
from all other creatures. This distinctive thing is the fact that
man stands in this double relationship between his king and his
neighbor. When he fails to occupy this double relationship, when
something is lacking here, then he is actually missing his life,
his destiny; then it ends in an abyss—just as our parable says.

First, what about the relationship to the king, to God? This
is a problematical thing. The parable says that "man"—this is
the best way to express it—owes the king millions of dollars. This
is an enormous sum. The only way he can meet it is to surrender
his own life and the lives of his family. In plain terms, this signifies
that to be in debt, to be a sinner means that we owe to God
everything we are and everything we have. Is it necessary to
illustrate this? Do not we all know very well what this means?
God created us. Therefore he can demand that we come back
to him exactly as we were when we left his hands. This is a
tremendous, a daunting statement.

What were we like when we left God's hands?

Well, he gave us *eyes* to see his glory. And, God save the mark, what have our eyes not beheld, what have they not lusted after, what sights have not defiled them!

He gave us our *mouths* and the gift of speech in order that we might praise him and communicate with our neighbor. And, God save the mark, what have these mouths not spoken and whispered and hissed! How many a curse has stood hard by a prayer; how often have these lips not denied, defamed, destroyed, desolated, distressed, put others to death!

He gave us our *hands* in order that they might serve and work and give help in his name and thus in all these things be lifted up to his glory. And, God save the mark, what have these hands not done! We shudder to describe their deeds.

And now God demands us back again, just as we were when we left his good and eternal hands. We ought for once to see very clearly what it would mean to be compelled to face a person who knows everything about us: every secret word, every dream in which the unconscious (but note that it is *my* unconscious) emerges, every real thought behind my polite words, every act under the cover of darkness. Before such a person we would want to disappear and sink into the ground. Anybody who has ever faced the question whether he should confess knows what a struggle it demands, what a death it is.

And what happens here is that a man actually stands before God and confesses everything to him and this turns out to be his death sentence. He not only feels like sinking into the ground, he actually does. No man can stand before God if he takes him seriously.

So when the king looks at this poor, corrupt fellow who has squandered his master's goods in evil machinations, lifts him up from the ground, takes his hand, absolves him, and gives him a new start, we can rightly appreciate this astonishing, incomprehensible reaction of the king only if we see it against the dark foil of the fact that the whole scene should have turned out altogether differently. There is certainly nothing logical about it. What is logical is what the culprit did to his fellow servant:

he made him pay back his debt, his incomparably smaller debt. Sin and retribution belong together. This is logical.

And then the miracle happens. God snatches us out of this terrible logic and simply says, "You shall be my child again." And he says this not because he was easygoing, not because he was indifferent and couldn't be hard—the conclusion of the parable shows how infinitely hard and consistent God can be. When Bodelschwingh lost his four children in a diphtheria epidemic he said, "Now for the first time I know how hard God can be." No, God is not soft. Nor should we be soft and let our fellow men get away with everything in the name of forgiveness. The Christian dare not be the point of least resistance in the world. Very often there must be some objective, matter-of-fact reckoning. Even the king in our parable does some reckoning and is objective about it. There is no concealing, no covering up the fact that the wicked servant embezzled ten million dollars.

But this is the wonderful part of it: God seeks you and me with such an everlasting love that, despite all the calculating and all the objectivity, he sees, not the "object," but back of the object his unhappy "child," not only the values but also the person, that when he condemns the sin he does not condemn us, that though he calls sin by its name, he also calls me by my name, and calls me his child.

And when his Son dies on the cross we get some idea of what it costs him to beat down the logic of his holy righteousness and remain our Father. Truly, this is no "kindly God" who covers everything with the mantle of his love; this is no harmless metaphysical concept; this is the holy, subduing God who breaks the cursed spell of relentless logic and gives us the miracle of sonship.

What must have been this man's state of mind when he left this scene of clemency and pardon? A short time before, he was a depressed man. The suffocating realization that sooner or later the time of reckoning must come accompanied him like a shadow. It made the costly carpets, which he had secured with the embezzled millions, burn beneath his sandaled feet; it gave the champagne a searing, sour taste; it made him wake up at night in a cold sweat.

And now all this—the fear, the shame, the pangs of conscience —was gone, blown away without a trace. Now he departed richer than he had ever been before, for he had experienced the ineffable goodness of the king. He had never know that before. He learned that it can be nothing short of delight, that it can be simply wonderful to be able to trust someone with one's whole heart and love him in gratitude. To live by forgiveness is actually to experience a transport of joy and relief. Compared with this, all the substitute joys he had bought with his dishonest money were mere trifles. Now, for the first time, he knew what life really means. Indeed, I venture to assert that only the person who at some time has experienced release from all the burden of conscience really knows what joy is—a businessman who doesn't have to worry any more over the dubious yarns he has concocted in making out his tax returns, even though it means some material losses; the young person who is no longer condemned and oppressed by wild passion and temper and now feels the Lord's hand gripping his own. These people simply know that happiness has been bestowed upon them, that almost incredible good fortune has befallen them.

But now our story takes a sudden and appalling turn. It turns out that man is terribly at odds with himself and that in the very next moment the inspiring, reviving stream of life can be poisoned and turned into a noisome sump. No sooner has the central figure in our parable returned to ordinary life, after leaving the Sunday atmosphere that obtained in that audience at the palace, than the blessed experience is obliterated.

There he meets a poor wretch to whom he had once made a small loan; a few pennies, in any case the merest trifle compared with what *he* had owed to his master. He may even have extended this credit from the funds he had embezzled and not from his own pocket. Mr. X, as we may call the unmerciful servant, is suddenly in the same relation to his fellow servant as the king was in relation to him just a few moments before. Except that now the situation is far more insignificant; it is only a matter of a few paltry pennies. But now he treats his fellow servant in exactly the opposite way from that in which his master treated him.

He simply allows the logic of retribution to run its full course. Nobody can blame him, for, after all, when he demands repayment of the money he is acting in accord with the principles of justice. Of course his fellow servants were outraged by the harshness of the punishment he inflicted. But this is only a human sentiment. There is no real objection that can be made to it. Is this really so? Well, the fact is that you can have no objection to it whatsoever so long as you remain on the level of human society with its legal rules of the game, so long as you fail to take into account that one invisible factor, which is involved in this situation no matter what you say, the fact that this man has had dealings with God, and that what he experienced in relation to God—if it was a genuine reality—must also become operative in his own life, in his vocation, in his company, in his relations to his associates and neighbors.

Mr. X is reacting according to the law of retaliation, the principle of: You hit me, so I hit you; you owe me, so I collect. This is human and legal. But Mr. X has forgotten (you have forgotten!) that he has just been accepted by God contrary to all expectation, and that now he must live in response to the mercy he has received and stop responding to the injustice that men do to him. We are always responding to something; the question is *what* are we responding to?

This is the question, and none other, that determines whether we are disciples of Jesus. This is by no means determined only by faith. We should not misunderstand Paul and Luther. After all, Mr. X, too, believed and trusted and availed himself of forgiveness. But his life was not a response to this event; in practice his life remained on the level of reaction to men. And therefore his faith immediately passed into decay and was eaten by worms. How much worm-eaten, vile-smelling faith lies on the carrion heaps of Christendom! And the children of this world are quick to sense the odor of it. These are the kind of Christians who attend an audience of the King every day, or at least every Sunday, in order to cadge a bit of forgiveness and grace, and then fail to see the beggar on the very steps of the palace. Outside the door they act just the opposite from the way the King has just dealt with them. They are fanatics for justice when it profits their egoism, and they are fanatics for grace and pseudo children of God when it is a question of getting God to clear away their own misery.

What a terrible self-contradiction, what abominable hypocrisy! It simply makes our Christianity unworthy of belief. God must put up with our despising him, but anybody who despises us must suffer the consequences. We are constantly rebelling against God. When something happens in our life which we do not understand or when things go wrong we immediately begin to sulk: "How can God permit such a thing?" But when somebody rebels against *us*, reproaches us, and does not understand us, we get peeved. For God we have very little time, very little room in our hearts, and usually no money. But woe to the person who pays no attention to us, woe to him who ignores us—he'll pay for it! We are always judging by two different standards. That we should be forgiven and exempt from the law of retribution, that we should be given another chance by God, this is only right and proper. After all, this is God's "line," that's what he's there for. But *we* go on treating our debtors as before. This is *our* line—this is the human, all-too-human element in us and we are all too ready to flirt with it. But such is the way of the world.

But now it turns out that God won't stand for it. Forgiveness which is not passed on to others is an abomination to him. He takes it back again.

When God forgives us, this is a chance, an opportunity, nothing more. A chance is a limited probation. God has affirmed with the blood of his Son, with his heart's blood, that he loves me, that I may be his child, and that my conscience may be free. This is, so to speak, the agreement which he offers me. But now I must ratify the agreement. And the way I ratify it—and the *only* way I ratify it—is by taking what God has given to me and passing it on to others. If I do not do this, I contradict the terms of the agreement by my own life and practice, and thereby nullify the agreement. We may perhaps have a copy of the New Testament in our pocket or at any rate at home. That New Testament is the agreement. But we have nothing but a worthless piece of paper in our pocket if we do not ratify it. No, I must correct myself; we have in our pocket not merely a worthless piece of paper, but an indictment. Everything that God has done for me becomes an indictment if I do not allow this act of God to flow through me to others. For then I have embezzled the mercy of God; then suddenly I am millions of dollars in debt; then I have allowed Jesus to die in vain. Then I am a murderer. Yes, that's what it says: "In anger his lord delivered him to the jailers, till he should pay all his debt." Where am I, really? Could it be that I myself am marching, with the New Testament in my pocket and this sermon ringing in my ears, to my jailers?

So Peter has the answer to his question of when the limit has been reached, when a man can stop being patient and forgiving and may with good conscience explode. This answer can be summed up in this way:

First: Your question, Peter, is completely wrong. For it starts with the assumption that it is a moral hardship, a colossal exertion of self-control for you to grant pardon repeatedly to another person. It is true that it may look this way at first. Even when somebody tramps on your toes at a turnstile and then adds insult to injury by saying, "Watch your step," it is much easier to hiss at him or tramp on his toes in return. It is a wonderful relief to let off steam and "let him have it on the nose." It is a trying thing to hold on to oneself, to put the brakes on the natural tendency to react, and swallow one's anger. But when we look at things this way we are shifting then to the moral level and that makes it all wrong. As soon as we mention the subject of "self-control," forgiveness becomes a function of the will.

Then quite naturally—with all this repeated pardoning and incessant forbearing—we must assume that there will be fatigue and exhaustion of the will. Forgive more than seven times—no, this is really too much of a strain, if we apply the standard of will power.

Jesus, however, shifts us completely beyond this level of morality and says to us: If in all seriousness you consider how often you have offended God and how he has forgiven you again and again; if you take seriously the literal fact that every morning and every night you can say, "Forgive us our debts," and that he actually does forgive them; then it is no longer, in any case not primarily, a question of "self-control" whether you go on repeatedly forgiving your neighbor. Therefore, please, when your neighbor does something bad, do not say, "Now as a Christian I must grin and bear it; now I mustn't react like a natural man; now I must snap to attention spiritually and maintain an attitude of forbearance." When you do this as a Christian you are right back on the moral level again. And, besides, to do this only produces repressions and complexes, nor is the other person made any happier by this kind of forbearance.

No, the glorious thing is that with Jesus we become free, at ease, and cleansed of complexes. In these cases we do not alert the will but quietly utter this simple prayer: "Lord, how often hast thou not forgiven *me*; how often hast thou not taken *me* back again! Thou didst suffer even bitter death that I might become and remain a child of God. Thou wilt not now let me become an unmerciful servant toward this my neighbor who owes me these few trifles." It is not a matter of exerting great will power; it is rather a matter of turning our eyes very slightly and looking at the Cross. Then the will will function of itself. It is "added unto us." Then we shall not so easily grow weary. "As we have received mercy, we do not grow weary" (II Cor. 4:1 Luther's rendering). For God has not grown weary of us either.

The second thing we have learned is this: No matter how miserably we fail, no matter how choked with resentment toward our neighbors, our family, our close associates we may become, our first question should not be whether our nerves will fail and whether our self-control will be equal to these trials, but rather whether we ourselves have sufficiently availed ourselves of the forgiveness of God. Only he who himself receives forgiveness can pass on forgiveness. One doesn't go far on one's nerves when in reality the spiritual man in us is sick. When a person grows weary of forgiving he has not yet availed *himself* sufficiently of mercy.

And finally, the third thing we have learned: We receive the liberating gift of forgiveness only if we pass it on immediately. These two things, "Forgive us our debts" and "as we forgive our debtors," belong together. Forgiveness is like the wand in a relay race; it must be passed on. If a man keeps on running, clutching it to himself, he is sure to break down. It is of the very essence of this wand that it exists to be passed on. It is the foolishness of the unmerciful servant that he violated this elementary rule and thus brought shipwreck upon himself.

Should there be one among us who is oppressed by guilt and anxiety who simply cannot find peace and assurance of forgiveness, though he has yearned for it and prayed for it again and again, that person ought simply to forgive his brother and his sister and in the name of Jesus simply leave off this everlasting spitefulness. Perhaps the only reason for all his peacelessness lies in the fact that he has simply accepted all the sermons and meditations on grace and mercy which he has heard and stored them away in his heart like buried treasure. He may perhaps, secretly and behind closed shutters, count up all these divine securities and assurances of grace over and over again and still find no joy in it. They are nothing but dead spiritual capital. And finally he says—and quite rightly—"All this is nothing but worthless paper that doesn't help me one bit." God gives us real treasures; we are rich people, but only if we put this capital into use. Forgive your brother; then you will also get peace for yourself. Otherwise you are a dead spiritual capitalist.

And because all this is so, because grace is something that can decay, because forgiveness is a chance we can lose, therefore the blessedness of forgiveness is never far away from fear and trembling—always behind it there stands the dark foil of failure. In the ancient language of the church this means that the Law is always related to the Gospel as its counterpart. Grace is not cheap; it is not unemployed income.

Look at your neighbor, that neighbor who (as Luther once said) "would become a Christ to you," is standing at your door. Don't you feel your hand in the hand of God? But what is your other hand doing? Is it a clenched fist—or is it stretched out toward your neighbor so that the divine circuit can be closed and thus allow the current of creative power to flow into you? Our left hand is capable of doing something different from our right hand (in the same way that we may be "schizophrenic" in our minds and souls and belong to two masters). And this can split and break us. It can send us staggering down the wrong road and make us miss the gates of the Father's house. But to miss those gates means that I shall also lose myself and miss my destiny, that I shall not become what I was intended and created to be. For I was intended to be, not merely an echo of the world's evil and its exemplars (which so often get on my nerves), but rather to be an echo of that unceasing love that comes from the cross.

❧ 14 ❧

The Parable of the Importunate Widow

And he told them a parable, to the effect that they ought always to pray and not lose heart. He said, "In a certain city there was a judge who neither feared God nor regarded man; and there was a widow in that city who kept coming to him and saying, 'Vindicate me against my adversary.' For a while he refused; but afterward he said to himself, 'Though I neither fear God nor regard man, yet because this widow bothers me, I will vindicate her, or she will wear me out by her continual coming.'" And the Lord said, "Hear what the unrighteous judge says. And will not God vindicate his elect, who cry to him day and night? Will he delay long over them? I tell you, he will vindicate them speedily. Nevertheless, when the Son of man comes, will he find faith on earth?"

LUKE 18:1-8

This is another parable which we cannot read without being somewhat startled by the extraordinary daring of some of Jesus' comparisons.

On another occasion he compared God with an unjust steward, and here the no less dubious figure of a very capricious judge is made to serve as an illustration of God's attitude toward our prayers.

But this only adds one more link to the long chain of questions that surrounds the mystery of prayer. One of the many puzzles that confront us here consists in the fact that God is doing nothing less than offering to his praying church a part in his government of the world. We know the story that tells of the time when the fate of Sodom and Gomorrah was dependent upon ten righteous and one praying man (Gen. 18:20 ff.). We also remember the ancient account of Moses lifting up his hands in prayer during the battle between Israel and Amalek and how the course of the battle fluctuated according as he held them high or allowed them to drop in weariness (Exod. 17:11 ff.).

But what is the use of these old stories to us! When we think about the government of the world today we calculate the various power-constellations. We determine what ideological, economic, and military potential the men who make history have behind them. We inform ourselves as to how many divisions the East has and how many divisions the West possesses and the relative strength of rocket and steel production. After all, *these* are the real factors that play a role on the chessboard of history. The great *doers* seem to be the ones who do the job. Obviously, *they* are the ones who direct the game of power.

And here we are told, and we are expected to believe, that God invests the pray-ers with a share in the government of the world, that we are permitted to pray for peace, for favorable weather, for the reunification of our country, and for liberation from tyranny. And if this assertion that prayer is a world power is to be taken seriously (and if it is not to be taken seriously, then our faith would be futile and we should be of all men the most miserable and deluded), then this is a message that should make us tremble.

But something even more massive is still to come.

In the parable the praying church is presented in the figure of a widow to whom injustice has been done and who is completely helpless against her adversary. Even in the judge she runs into a stone wall of cold indifference. A widow is a woman who has lost the protection of a man and therefore may often be victimized. For most people are pitiless and cold enough to be impressed only by someone who has power behind him and can defend himself. A widow is often a negligible quantity, a nonentity that can be brushed aside.

Are we to believe then that this church, which is represented as a defenseless widow without manly protection, that this church which folds its hands in prayer as a sign of its defenselessness, that this church by its intercession before the throne of God actually shares in the government of the world and participates in the divine ordering of war and peace and curse and blessing? Is not this simply too fantastic to believe? But nothing less than this we are assured and promised.

Do we still remember when the bombs held sway, when our sons and husbands and brothers were pitilessly mowed down, when we were dragged defenselessly into the capitulation and the triumph of the world powers, do we still remember how, suddenly, the power of the pray-ers began to gleam like shining armor and how it began to dawn upon us that this power was more real than all the feckless maneuvers of the doers and all the so-called "real factors" in life? Do we still remember how we were comforted by Reinhold Schneider's sonnet as it circulated among us, copied a thousand times on crumpled bits of paper?

> Now only *pray-ers* shall stay the threatening sword
> That hangs, a parlous doom, above our head,
> • • • • • • • • • • • • • • • • • • •
> For *doers* cannot conquer heaven's Lord.
> What they unite will soon be riven, dead,
> What they renew, o'ernight will wane instead,
> Their works have only ruin for reward.

Were not all the doers and the so-called real factors cast in a play that Another was directing? Has a single one of all the doers in the world's history ever actually carried out a program in which he realized his own will? In the end, was not all that he did always deflected from its original course, taken out of his control and swept away by mysterious waves? Was he not himself on the program drawn up by *Another*—Another whom he never dreamed of, because he was always thinking only of himself? What did Cyrus and Nebuchadnezzar, what did Hitler and Stalin really know about their role in the drama which Another had written and was then staging, the last act of which will end before the throne of God at the coming of the Lord? The church of Jesus Christ is in truth a defenseless widow, and when it engages in ecclesiastical politics and strategy it never accomplishes much; this is nothing more than a feeble arrow launched at armored giants.

But one thing this church, this company of believers, does have. It has access to that Other who causes the unfolding of the drama of the world. And therefore it has a power greater than the magnificent and arrogant figures in gleaming armor who enter and leave the stage. In the end only Jesus Christ will be left upon the world's stage. Then it will be clear that in all the acts of this cosmic drama there is traceable a mysterious trend, an ordering tendency, that points to this great finale of history. And all those who considered themselves great, who made their entrances and exits and for a few moments were able to make us little people down in the pit of history hold our breath and set us trembling, all these could not in the end do anything else but bring on this *one* royal moment of God. They knew nothing about this finale, because they were under the delusion that they themselves were directing the drama of the world, whereas they were only supers and extras who were permitted to walk for a moment across the stage in grandiose costumes, only to disappear in the wings on the other side.

If we take the time to study the surrounding texts in which our parable is embedded, we shall note that they all refer to this last moment of history and that we cannot understand this story of the petitioning widow unless we see it in the light of this last day. The church of Christ is bidden to pray, "Thy kingdom come." And this means that it has *influence* upon this last day. And so likewise all the days preceding the last day, the first, second, and third acts of the world drama are committed to the church. For all these days are mysteriously ordered and directed toward the great triumph of God. The kingdoms of the world are passing, but the kingdom of God is coming. The congregation of Jesus has its hand, as it were, on the longer end of the lever and therefore it can afford to possess only the feeble arm of a widow. It can tip the lever with folded hands, whereas on the other, shorter side, the weight of all the world powers, the doers, and their divisions and millions of tons of steel production are not sufficient to budge it. For the poor widow stands at the strategic key-point of world history. She rests in the heart of God, and God has promised her that his heart will not be deaf to her pleadings. He who has influence upon the heart of God rules the world. The poor widow is truly a world power.

There is good reason then to take a look at *how* she prays. Perhaps this may clear up many things that strike us in this parable at first as being rather strange.

The first thing that strikes us about the praying of this woman is the incredible intensity with which she presents her petition. She is beset by people who are perhaps bent upon driving her from her house and home and threatening the life and welfare of her children. And now in this utmost distress she knows that nothing will do her any good, no appeal to her enemies, no clever move, nor even her own energy and ability by which she might hope to prevail against malicious fortune. There are situations in which none of this is of any help and probably there is nobody among us who has not at some time or other been in such a predicament. She knows that there is only one thing—actually, only one single thing!—that can help her, and that is to get this *one* man on her side. And this *one* man on his part needs to speak a *single* word and all her troubles will be over. In other words, one must knock on the right door; everything in life depends upon finding the right strategic point from which all the distressing and anxious situations can be mastered. Therefore the widow stakes everything on this *one* card, that of gaining the favor of this one man.

You have noticed, no doubt, how frequently in the last few

sentences I have repeated the words "this one" and "this one thing" —this one thing on which everything depends. And almost inevitably we think of the prayer-hymn: "One thing needful! then Lord Jesus, teach me this one thing to know!"

And this is precisely what our Lord is saying to us: If you were to take seriously, if *you* were to take seriously the fact that God reigns, that he holds in his hand your personal destiny as well as peace and war among the nations, and if you were also to take seriously the assurance that you have a voice in all this and that God will listen to you; if therefore you were to take seriously the fact that everything depends on this one thing and this One Man, then you *too* would keep dinning your prayers in the ears of God with this *same* persistence, this same stubbornness, this same intensity.

Which of us has ever even tried to make such an onslaught upon God? Which of us has ever once prayed a whole night through?

I know very well what some of you may be thinking as I venture to express all this in terms so gross and almost offensively blunt. You may think that this dinning of our prayers into the ears of God is simply lack of respect. This would be to take ourselves far too seriously. After all, we see this kind of thing in the pure human realm. When a petitioner keeps hounding us and sticking to us like a bur, he becomes a nuisance. We find this repulsive and finally even our good-naturedness begins to go on strike.

But with God it is quite different. Here the parallels on the parable let us down. In other words, when we keep pestering *him* this is not at all a sign of lack of respect, but rather a sign that we are taking him and his promises seriously, that we are taking him at his word. If Jesus Christ did not exist and if we had not seen by his cross that God loves us and that this love cost him something, that he allowed his own heart to be pierced for us, then, of course, all this would be megalomaniac presumption. How should a man of himself ever conceive the idea that God is interested in us? But, the cross being what it is, we can come in the name of this Man Jesus. And God rejoices when we do this, because then he knows that we understand his heart and that now we are no longer "pious" and superior but dare to come to him as helpless children.

In any case, however, it is sheer humbug and hypocrisy for us to say: "I will not come to God with my petty affairs; I will not pray to him for good weather for a picnic; I will not expect him to help me in my examinations. My Father in heaven knows anyhow what I need (after all, he is omniscient!); let his will be done." God has no pleasure in this kind of super-piety and this precocious, patronizing resignation, because then we are twisting his own words in our mouth.

In other words, anybody who, right from the start, before he really opens his mouth, says, "Thy will be done," no longer has any real trust in God at all. He is really saying in his heart, "Fate still runs its course; dear old God has retired to his sphere and has no intention of intervening on my account. And perhaps he himself is only a circumlocution, a personification of fate." The pious people who keep on saying in this way, "Thy will be done," are the very ones who are not taking seriously the fact that God has given his children a right to speak on everything that concerns them. They sit back in their unbelief and finally they do not even say, "Thy will be done" any more, but rather, "Everything that happens was bound to happen anyhow."

The petition, "Thy will be done," must never be the first petition in our prayers. So here we must be careful. As Luther once said, first I must open wide my apron, first I must boldly, heartily, and quite ingenuously speak out what I want to receive from my Father. This and nothing else is what he desires of us, for he no longer wants to be "God" at all (as we conceive of him), but rather our Father, with whom his children may speak freely and frankly, even foolishly. For is not what we so often ask for in our prayers actually the merest stuff and rubbish? In order to be able to present serious, worthy petitions I would really have to *know* what I need. And to know what I need I would have to be capable of correctly interpreting my own life and the lives of other people, indeed the life of the world itself. But can I do this? So, for example, I pray that I may get well, but in reality my most bitter need is to remain longer in the school of suffering. I pray that I may have a successful career or that I may win the sweepstakes, whereas God needs me in some altogether different place, and he knows that success and money would be poison to my character. In the midst of a war I pray for the gift of peace; but God knows that we must drink the cup to its dregs. Thus in my prayers I make all kinds of false diagnoses, false estimates, and false interpretations of the real situation. And therefore our prayers are often merely foolish talk.

But have we fathers and mothers ever taken it amiss when our children talked nonsense to us, when they asked us to buy them a horse or a Cadillac or a jet plane? Naturally, we could not grant these things, even if we had the money or were the emperor of America, because it would not be good for the children. And they very quickly become reconciled to our refusal to do so and hold no grudge against us because they know that we mean well by them.

So, after we have spoken frankly and openly in our prayer, we should draw a clear line at the end and then (but only then!) say, "Thy will be done; thou wilt do what is right and good; thou wilt choose what is right from all our foolish prayers. Thou knowest best what we really need."

Now do we understand why the widow keeps dinning her petition into the ears of the judge so persistently and incessantly? And therefore, again we ask the question: Which of us has ever tried this even once? Which of us has ever ventured even once to be so radical and consistent in taking God at his word that he *wants* us to pray to him and that he will choose what is right from *every* prayer we pray?

Secondly, the intensity with which the widow pleads with the judge—she "kept coming to him" repeatedly—is also related to the fact that the judge is an unjust judge, a man with a heart of stone. At any rate he is a man whose justice—to put it mildly—is not immediately apparent and not to be had at the first asking. If that had been the case, the widow would presumably not have had to come herself at all, and certainly not repeatedly. A brief court order would have been sufficient.

But it is precisely this *hidden* justice, this justice that is not immediately apparent, that spurs her on to go all out. And here again our Lord is giving us a hint; for God often *seems* to us to be just as dour, hard-hearted, and uninterested as this judge was in fact. Is he not constantly ignoring our wishes? Time and time again is not our praying like telephoning—Rilke once used this metaphor—when nobody answers at the other end or the other party suddenly hangs up just as we are about to state *our* business? Are we not being ruled by blind chance, without the slightest possibility of discovering any higher providence whatsoever? Is not Wolfgang Borchert right when he says at the end of his story of the girl who commits suicide, "It made no difference whether it was a glass tube that shattered or somebody's heart—God didn't hear it anyhow"?

When we have such experiences (and who hasn't had them!) we either resign ourselves, or we crack up, or we shake our fist in defiance of this leaden, taciturn heaven. But this very silence of the judge only prompts the widow to press her demands upon him even more vehemently.

May it not be that very often God remains silent in order that we shall not submit in fatalistic resignation, and content ourselves with the cheap snap judgment that says, "Whatever happens must happen"; but rather in order that we may learn to remain in communication, in constant contact with him? God's grace is not cheap; it is not handed out for a mere song. God loves those who take the kingdom of heaven by force (Matt. 11:12). They are the only ones who then have their experiences with God and know what they have in having him. This is what Kierkegaard meant when he said that God is always entering incognito; he makes himself uncertain and even ambiguous to us, in order that we may be plunged into a concern for him, into an agitated and searching uncertainty and thus there be aroused in us the "infinite passion of inwardness." This can be true even in ordinary life, for when I am all too sure of a person whom I love, my passion for him begins to cool. Even in love the cheap certainties, the relationship in which there is no doubt and concern, are dangerous. May not God therefore often wait and remain silent in order to make me seek him more passionately and persistently? Was not this the case not only with the oppressed widow but also the Canaanite woman?

Moreover, in life, too, it is often true that the people who mean the most to us are not the amiable charmers, with whom we establish contact at first sight; rather it is with the very people who make it hard for us and whom we learn to know only after repeated painful attempts that the deepest and most fruitful relationships result. But then we know, too, what we really have in them. Even in God's silence and his refusing to give himself easily there is a hidden goodness. He only wants us to seek him more passionately; and all the while he has long since found us.

But as soon as we put it in this way it becomes apparent how completely and utterly different is our heavenly Father from this judge. The judge is in actuality what God only appears to be to our feeble faith. The judge finally relented only because the widow kept hammering at him until he was literally softened up and because he was afraid that she might even begin raving at him.

"How much more," says the Lord, "will not your Father in heaven, who is really just, vindicate his elect, who cry to him day and night?" And he says this not without a grain of irony: You so-called believers, you immediately give up if God isn't on the spot to comply at once to the first whisper of your prayers, when all the while, if he tarries a while with his comfort, he is only waiting to see whether we shall continue to be faithful to him. That's what you do! And now look at this widow, who had a completely different person to deal with and still did not give up. She had to crack open a heart that was as hard as a safe. And you have only to open unlocked doors when you pray to God. This widow should put you to shame.

Thirdly, we must consider one final essential feature in our parable. The whole parable is directed toward the day of judgment and closes with the question, "Will the Son of Man, when he returns, find faith on earth?" Or will all the people have fallen asleep? In other words, watching, waiting and praying belong together. One who prays, stays awake.

Here we people of today will have to change our ideas considerably if we are going to understand this. We think that the only person who is awake and watchful is the one who is "alive," who keeps his eyes open on the job, watches his chances, is constantly on the go and always a nose ahead of his competition, and is therefore exhibiting incessant activity. But this is just the kind of person who, in a very deep sense, may be sleeping and dreaming.

This is shown, for example, by that phenomenon which has come to be called executive's disease. People who are overactive, people who are constantly loaded with tension, one day may be hit by the familiar circulatory disturbances and heart attacks.

But the trouble with these people is by no means confined to this pathological high tension and activity. It lies far more in the fact that with all their frantic activity they have forgotten and dreamed away the real and ultimate question of their lives. And finally in despair they ask themselves, "What's the use of it all? What's the use of this everlasting grind? Why am I really filling my barns? What am I going to do with success, and where am I driving in my Cadillac?" One can, you know, not only *run* away from oneself, but also *drive* away from oneself, whether it be on a motorcycle or in a sports car. The "wings of the morning" with which we flee to "the uttermost parts of the sea" have long since been mechanized and become a part of our technical inventory.

And because we are made miserable by this question and the possibility that despite all our success we may have missed the meaning of our life, we plunge all the more madly into our business in order to anesthetize ourselves—which means, put ourselves to sleep. So people go on dreaming, though outwardly they may look like wide-awake realists and executives whom nobody could easily bamboozle.

When the rich fool heard the voice saying, "This night your soul is required of you," he was suddenly aware that he had dreamed his life away. Here was a man who never missed a trick, who took into account even the smallest details, and yet he dreamed away the fact that everything depends on this one night, when he must appear before God.

And now the Lord says to us: The man who prays (not the man who works only, but the man who prays) is the man who stays awake, who does not dream and confuse the big things with the small things, but retains a wide-awake and realistic sense of the real proportions of life. The man who prays knows that there is only one thing that really counts and that is getting straight with God. The man who prays also loses the anxiety of life because he knows that, despite all the tricks and whims of fortune, history will end according to plan, and that nothing can happen to us except what he has foreseen and what is for our good. But when our anxiety is taken away from us, then we shall have no more anxiety-dreams either; then we shall be stabbed broad awake. A man who is straight with God has peace in his heart and therefore he can be simple and realistic in life. For anxiety-dreams and worries are poor counselors. A person who is anxious puts a false estimate on everything. He trembles at a straw because he thinks it is a falling beam, and he is toppled by a beam because he thought it was a straw. The man who prays is recalled from his anxiety-dream into reality, for he has the measure of eternity and the day of judgment and that gives him his sense of proportion.

The man who prays will also be released by God from many of the diseases of tension. For God takes from him the care and the concern for the morrow and gives him instead the poise and the peace of the man who looks to the last day—that day when God will celebrate his triumph, and everything that for us shortsighted people is now blown up into such disproportionate pseudo importance will be reduced to its relative place.

We understand then why Jesus' parable concludes with this question of whether there will be those who pray here on earth when he comes again. One thing is sure: our prayers are heard above. But are there petitioners here below? *That* is the problem, not whether our prayers are heard, but whether there are any who pray. We men keep asking, "Where is there a God who hears me?" Which of the two is right? In any case, he will come again when days and hours are done. But what will things look like then?

Will the lamps of the virgins be extinguished; will a great darkness lie upon the face of the earth with only the skeletons of deserted cathedrals rising above it? Will the trumpets of judgment speak only to a great silence, because God has been consigned to nothingness by the silence and sleep of men? Or will God find here and there in this darksome world a gleam of shining light? Will he find the burning lamps by which he recognizes those who pray, by which he sees that there is one who has been waiting and has not fallen asleep as he stood still, or as he kept running about? Will I be one of these points of light which are so helpful in this dark world—not only because this is the way God finds us but also because they are signs and signals for men, our fellow men, to show that God is coming and that for God's sake they must remain awake?

It may perhaps be nothing more than scientific fantasy, yet it might be a good spiritual exercise for us to imagine how atomic physics could one day bring self-judgment upon our earth, how it could destroy all life and turn our planet into a scattered dust cloud in the universe. Then everything would be suddenly and utterly ended. Then the chime of Mozart would be no more and the sound of Beethoven's *Missa Solemnis* would have died away forever. And every lilting verse and lovely song would be blown to nothingness—as well as the songs of birds and the starry heavens and the shining of a spring morning. "And the sea was no more," says an ancient prophecy (Rev. 21:1). Indeed, even the memory of all this would be extinguished, for there would no longer be anybody to remember.

What then would be left? What could be left except that ongoing life with God that once began in prayer and nevermore can cease (whatever place God may provide for it)? What else could there be except our names, written in heaven and stored in a fireproof treasury? What else but this could ever survive this fire?

The Lord concludes his parable with a question. And this meditation, too, shall end with a question: "Am I one of those points of light to which God can come? Do I bear that fireproof Name?" He who has ears to hear, let him hear!

❧ 15 ☙

The Meaning of Life

I know of no better model by which to illustrate the meaning of life than Jesus' parable of the prodigal son (Luke 15). If we are to do this, we certainly dare not interpret this story moralistically, as if it were a story about a misguided young man who ran away from his father—into the Foreign Legion, as it were, but in any case into a foreign land—and was completely ruined, but in the last moment picked himself up again. This story has a meaning that is totally different from that of a merely moral lesson; indeed, it has so many levels of meaning that one can hardly exhaust it. And today I should like to bring out only one of these many meanings.

So here is a young man who asks his father for his inheritance in order that he may go off to some unknown foreign country.

Why does he want to go away?

It need not have been an obscure desire for adventure that drove him away. If that were the case, would his father have been so ready to pay over his inheritance and let him go with so little fuss?

The young man undoubtedly went away to find himself. In order to be able to find oneself one must often go one's own way.

After all, at home, in the atmosphere of the parental house, he always had to do what the *father* wished or what the custom of the household required. There he always felt dependent. He could not do what *he* wanted to do, but only what was proper. Therefore he never belonged to himself, but to the conventions and the rules of his parental home. And then, too, because he was only the younger brother, he never got a chance to develop in his own way.

So he went away to find himself. One might also say that he went away to learn to know freedom. And this freedom that was so attractive to him, which promised that now for once he could really be "himself," this freedom seemed to him to be freedom from all ties whatsoever.

But then the story goes on to tell us something remarkable. It tells us that the lost son squandered all his substance with the wrong kind of friends, questionable women, and other evil company, that he was finally reduced to begging, deserted by everybody, and in the end was obliged to tend swine and eat with them.

So if at the start there was a certain touch of idealism in his departure, and he was driven by something like a yearning for freedom, he soon failed miserably. He sought freedom and soon found himself enslaved to his passions, to his ambition, to the fear of loneliness, which made him content with any companion who came along; he was enslaved to Mammon, by means of which he pandered to his own passions. Therefore he was not free; he was only bound and shackled in a different way. But this bondage was more dreadful than any bonds he had ever complained about at home.

What had happened? Well, quite simply this: quite contrary to what he had intended to do, he did not find himself; rather, he lost himself. When he set out he thought he would surely find himself if only he could allow all his abilities and talents to develop. And the fact is that he really could have developed himself in the "free" far country. But, as it turned out, what was it that did develop when his abilities were given free reign? Was it his so-called better self, his idealistic motives that came into play? Well, perhaps all this played its part too. But, in any case, in his self-development the *dark* sides of his nature also developed: his passions, his ambition, his fear, his sensuality. Because he developed himself, he became enslaved to precisely those dark powers which were within him and which developed along with everything else within him. And the end was that he found himself in the utter misery of servitude. Suddenly he was the lowest servant of all.

And now comes the second remarkable thing about this story. As he sat there in the misery of servitude he yearned for the freedom he had enjoyed as a son in his father's house. Suddenly he realized that that was real freedom. Yes, and he realized even more: he suddenly knew that freedom is not freedom from ties and obligations, but rather only a particular *way* of being bound. I have freedom only as the child of my father. I have freedom only when I live in accord with my origin, which means, when I am at peace with God. So when he resolved to go back home this was not a moral decision in which he persuaded himself to give up this wonderful, fascinating far country—with all the difficulty and depression that usually accompanies such decisions. No, this was a rightabout-face that was filled with trembling joy and the splendor of hope.

Now surely you will understand from all that has been said why I have called this story a fundamental contribution to the question of the meaning of life. For I shall find that meaning only if I find the *fulfillment* of my life; in other words, only if I realize what I was created and meant to be.

And this is exactly what happened to the prodigal son. In all his wanderings, which were supposed to lead him to himself, it was borne in upon him that the very time when he did *not* find himself was the time when he was seeking himself, but that he came to himself only when he came to the father. And the reason for this is that by nature man is *not* a cast form which needs only to develop in life, which has within it all the basic endowments that need only to grow. Man is rather a child of God who realizes himself only when he grows into this relationship of sonship to God, and this sonship to God fails of realization when he seeks to be an isolated self and acts like a soloist in the art of living.

Perhaps some of you who read this have seen those Gothic pictures in which a man is set before the background of a golden heaven. It is this background that suggests the really unique thing about this man, namely, that he is related to the glory of God. Today one would portray the unique thing about a man by emphasizing his individual characteristics and thus giving him strongly expressive features—naturally, only if he has them!— and thus accentuating what is "within" him. But this is precisely what the Gothic painters did not do. The faces have no individuality; gestures, poses, and drapery are strongly stylized. They were not concerned with individuality at all, in any case not primarily. And some art critics suggest that at this time individuality had not yet been "discovered." This is, to be sure, not altogether wrong, but still it addresses itself only to a symptom and not to the real reason for this form of portrayal. In other words, the individuality had not yet been discovered because they did not seek the unique thing in a man in his peculiar, individual self-development, but rather in the fact that he was related to the glory of God.

In doing this these painters were trying to say that the mystery and the meaning of human life lies not in his inherited structure and his characteristic abilities, but rather in what comes from outside of himself, in his relationship to him from whom our life comes and to whom it is going.

We receive the freedom to be ourselves only when we become free for God and open to God. And because this freedom and openness to God, this Father-child relationship, is given to us in Jesus Christ, it is really true that "If the Son makes you free, you will be free indeed." And then that other statement, "The truth will make you free," is also true. For the truth that is meant here is not the correctness of some dogmatic statement. It is rather a fact of our *lives*, namely, that we are existing in dependence upon the Father. Only he who has found the Father finds himself.

But then this means that provision has already been made to see that all that is original and unique in us may be fulfilled and realized, and therefore that our individuality is not neglected. For he who lives and breathes in the freedom of the Father's house, and hence has peace, will also be at peace with himself, because then nothing can separate him from the love that has taken hold of him, he no longer needs to have any fear of himself, even of the dark sides of his self. For now there is Someone with whom he is safe, Someone who is faithful to him, Someone to whom he can come just as he is.

We find life only if we find *this* life. But if we miss it, we shall fail to be what we were intended to be. We may even achieve greatness in the world; we may lack nothing in the way of outward goods; people may bow to us with deep respect; but we shall have missed the meaning of our life.

When the father embraced his homecoming son, then the son was not only at home again; he had also found himself. It was doubtless a deep prescience that this is really true that made the poet utter that beautiful line: "Blessed are those who are homesick, for they shall come home"—they shall find themselves.

❧ 16 ❧

Our Prayers

In our prayers, exactly as in our faith, we need not be anything but what we are; on the contrary, we need only be completely what we are. Whether we are sorrowful and in distress or laughing and inclined to feel sure of ourselves, we must approach God just as we are and put ourselves in his hands. Prayer, therefore, must never be thought of as a kind of insurance which is added to our concern, in the sense that our *concern* performs the function of devising a comprehensible remedy for our difficulty, and the prayer is then an additional attempt to cover our rear in the incomprehensible case that it might be of some importance to God. This would be a gross misunderstanding of prayer. To pray in need does not mean to whistle in the dark like a child and still go on anxiously peering into the dark to see what menace it may bring forth. We are not merely making a psychological observation, but expressing a thought that is connected with the very essence of prayer, when we say that this peering into the darkness paralyzes the wings of prayer, just as Peter's look at the waves paralyzed him, even though—and this is a parable for all who pray—he was eager to rush into the hands of his Lord.

What prayer is in this respect—namely, that it faces need

realistically and accepts it as being real and tangible, that it calls a spade a spade and mentions hunger and fear by name, but nevertheless proceeds to put all this in the hands of God—this is made very clear in the Lord's Prayer. That is to say, there are three things in the Lord's Prayer which turn my gaze away from myself.

First, in my praying I must not wish to perform an act in the sense of a performance by virtue of which I put myself in the center of things. I must not, for example, "heap up empty phrases" or "prattle" (as Luther put it), but rather "speak" as one would speak with one's father. But when one speaks to one's father, one does not gaze into a mirror, but rather one looks at *him* (Matt. 6:7).

Second, when I pray I do not think of myself as an individual alone in this world, but rather as being in the fellowship of *all* believers and all who pray. That's why I say *"our* Father." This word "our" indicates that every prayer takes place in a twofold "space," in two dimensions. First this "space" consists, figuratively speaking, in one's "closet," one's own inner chamber (Matt. 6:6). This image indicates *one* of the two dimensions which determine my life with God. Before God I am in some measure always an "individual" and to that extent nobody can take my place. In all the decisive things of our life—specifically the "distresses" of life—we actually stand alone; every man suffers his own illness, his own particular cares, his own death, and every man bears his sin completely alone. It is impossible for Adam to share his sin with Eve or for Eve to share it with the serpent or for one to shove it off upon the other. Or, rather, there is only *One* who bears all this with us and for us, and this One is not a man like us. Therefore this One is also the only one who shares the solitude of our prayer and is with us in the utter privacy of the "closet." This is precisely the meaning of prayer "in the name of Jesus" (cf. John 14:13-14; 15:16; 16:23, 24, 26, etc.). We may also express the meaning of this prayer in this way: in that "closet" the Word of God is with me, the judging, fatherly, condescending, and—so far as my own conviction is concerned—the crucified Word. I am alone with this Word; *it is the ground on which I stand and the name in which I come when I raise my voice.*

On the other hand, however, there is a second dimension: this "closet" is only a niche in the cathedral of the *whole* church—that church which is present wherever two or three are gathered together "in his name," and which is at the same time the church of all believers all the way from the patriarchs and prophets and apostles to the choir of the redeemed and the kingdom to come beyond our death. What binds all these together, beyond every individual concern expressed in their prayers, is the *praise* of God. Therefore the praise of God is really *the* function of prayer which holds the church together, for in *that* prayer we are one with the patriarchs and the people of the Last Day, "with angels and archangels and with all the company of heaven," however we may differ in the personal concerns and petitions of our prayers. Praise bursts the bounds of the "closet"; in praise I stand in the midst of the chorus of the praying church, the choir of the holy, universal, Christian church. That's why I begin my prayer by saying, "*Our* Father." When I say "our" I strike the note of praise.

Third, this has already suggested the third characteristic that determines the structure of the Lord's Prayer, and that is that its petitions are inlaid in this praise. I must go by way of the praise of God if I want to become a petitioner who is really speaking to *God* and not going in the wrong direction. I must praise his *name*, the coming down of his *kingdom*, and the holiness of his *will* before I can allow my attention to slip back to myself and begin to "petition." It is true that these first clauses of the Lord's Prayer are called "petitions," but actually they are rather praise, because I pray to God that his glory may become known. Moreover, the Lord's Prayer also ends in praise and adoration. At the close my attention turns away from myself and turns once more to the center, in order that in my concern about the gifts I have prayed for I may not forget the Giver, in order that I may remember that the theme of all prayer is the *hand* of God and not the pennies in that hand. Just as the *First* Commandment was intended to shine through all the rest of the Commandments, so the individual petitions of the Lord's Prayer are meant to be transparencies of the glory of God which are extolled at the beginning and the close of

the Prayer. And just as the fulfillment of the individual commandments should be fundamentally nothing else but our "fearing and
loving God," so God must be "praised" throughout all the individual petitions of the Lord's Prayer. The goal of all prayer is
always God himself; and if there is any criterion of prayer, and
above all any criterion by which we may criticize our own prayers,
it is this: There is not only a "First *Commandment*," but also a
"first *prayer*."

This thought that the praise of God is the ultimate theme of all
prayer makes it clear that our *petitionary* prayers, too, must always
be aimed at bringing our will into oneness with the will of God.
It would be presumptuous to want to force God's will down to
ours instead of uniting our will with his. This would only mean
that we distrusted his gracious condescension to the crib and to
the cross. No, the Father is already at our side as our Lord and our
Brother; he is already down in the depths from which we cry, and
here below, where he already *is*, we ought to unite our wills with
his, which means that we should trust that his will goes far beyond
what our will may ask or think, or better and more accurately,
that he descends to the depths and is near to us. This is really
what the petition, "Thy will be done," is saying to us. It is true
that this petition sets a limitation upon our prayer, but only in the
very definite sense that this limitation results, not from any
surmise concerning the external possibilities of its fulfillment, but
rather from the inside, from faith itself. This means that we trustfully lay our will in the hands of God and leave it to that hand to
grant our petitions or to set limits upon them. The emphasis lies
on the word "trustfully," for we go on praising the will of God no
matter what he may do about our will. And how else could we
praise his will except by trusting its goodness!

After we have thus poured out all that is in our hearts, after
we have spoken like beloved children with a loving father, we
draw, as it were, a thick line beneath it and write: "There, now we
have said all that we think. Do thou with it what *thou* thinkest
best; for thou art good and we are safe with thee." That, and
nothing else, is what is meant by "Thy will be done."

❦ 17 ❦

Who Am I?

I once found myself in the company of a number of automobile owners, all of them singing the praises of their cars. One said, "I have a car that can easily maintain a speed of a hundred and twenty miles an hour on the throughway." Another said, "And you should have seen the way my car went up that mountain! I tell you there wasn't a bit of steam or overheating, while all the big cars had to stop by the side of the road to cool off." A girl who knows she has an attractive profile and shows it off could not have been more conceited than these car owners. They acted as if these cars of theirs were *themselves* and thus were boasting about *themselves*.

The second experience of this kind was the following. I once said to a student, "You are really a gifted young man." He immediately blushed, as if I had praised him. I then said to him, "You don't need to blush, for I did not say that you are a splendid person or a wonderful fellow. I merely said that *gifts* have been bestowed upon you for which you are responsible to another who gave them to you. So *you* don't need to blush at all."

These two stories are characteristic because they illustrate the following fact about people. Man has the very noticeable tendency to latch on, so to speak, to everything that adds to his standing and enhances his social prestige, no matter whether it be a car or some position of economic or political power or his own intellectual abilities, and to identify himself with them and thus say: "This is I."

I could go on, however, and also tell you of cases in which one says to oneself: "This I am *not*." Here is a defendant who must answer to the charge of murder in a criminal trial. He and his attorney make every effort to show that it was the environment in which he grew up, his bad parental home, his unfortunate bringing-up that encouraged, nay, actually caused this, and that because of this he is therefore, to some extent at least, exonerated.

Or here is another situation. I wake up one morning horrified by a dream I have had. In the dream I committed an act so monstrous that I must surely be put in jail for it. Involuntarily I ask myself: "Is it really possible that such a murderer, such a hate-filled intriguer lurks within me?" The next moment, however, I say to myself: "No, that isn't I at all. This is just something inside of me, it's my unconscious, and, after all, these depths in my heart are covered up by my pure white, respectable vest."

We might also mention the story of Adam and Eve where the situation was exactly the same, and this may serve as our third illustration. After both of them had taken the forbidden fruit and thus trespassed against God by their disobedience, they were confronted by God. Adam said, "The woman whom thou gavest to be with me, she gave me the apple." And Eve said, "The serpent did it." So each was saying: "I am not identical with my action. I am merely the result, the product of factors *outside* of myself, factors over which I have no control."

The essence of these observations may be summarized as follows: I identify myself with everything that is good and beautiful and positive in my life. I say: "This is what I am," whether it is talents or a good car or my bank account that are involved. On the other hand, I dissociate myself from everything that is incriminating, everything that is shocking or dubious in my life, and I say: "This I am not."

Now, one of the most astounding and staggering transformations that we must go through as Christians is that in both cases we must learn to turn this completely around. The Sermon on the Mount, for example, penetrates and illuminates what is behind our respectable white vest. The Sermon on the Mount does not say: "Yes, my dear fellow, you are your white vest." It says rather: "You are what is underneath your white vest." And what is wrong there? Well, here is an example:

In the Sermon on the Mount Jesus Christ is taking issue with the ancient commandment, "You shall not kill." Now, presumably none of us is a murderer, and therefore we complacently conclude that this lets us out. But he goes on to say that not only the person who stabs another is a murderer but also one who is "merely" angry with his brother is a murderer. In other words, he is telling us that we have within us the *disposition* to murder, that we go through the first stages of an act of murder, and that these are *our*, or, more correctly, these are *my* thoughts that make me a murderer. Quite in accord with this, Adalbert Stifter, the very author in whose works only good people and an ordered world seem to appear, said that every one of us has within him a tigerlike tendency, and we never know what we might be capable of in a nervous fever that removes the inhibitions of our normal and conscious life.

This may sound extreme and even destructive and one might well ask: "How can a man live with such a philosophy of life?" And yet the one who uttered the Sermon on the Mount is actually trying to give us comfort by what he is saying; he is trying to give us some totally new impulses for our life.

When he addresses us at that point which is behind our white vest, at the point where we are murderers and adulterers, what he is saying to us is this: "Look here, I know how things are with you. I came down from headquarters in heaven and went into the dirtiest front-line trenches where you are fighting and struggling with others and with yourselves. I know what it is; I have gone through it myself. After all, I had to go through three satanic temptations; I have stood on the same battleground that you have.

And my heart trembled too when I was there. But now I have
something to tell you. In my Father's house in heaven there is no
office where the white vests that admit you to heaven are collected.
No, what you will find there will be tables decked for a feast, and
at those tables I shall be sitting with my brother men. And all of
them are very dubious fellows, just like you. But that's the Good
News. You can come and you will be accepted—just as you are.
You won't need to cover up with that white vest any more. You
will be loved and welcomed, just as you are, even *underneath* that
white vest. For, after all, you will be coming as my brothers. I'm
the one who is bringing you to the banquet. And, believe me, it
was no easy thing for me to reclaim you, to 'wake you up' and
pry you loose."

But we must also learn to turn our thinking completely around
in the *other* direction too. We related the examples of the automobile and the young man's talents and said that we human beings
tend to identify ourselves with all the positive things that enrich
our life. And this *too* is changed when we become Christians.
Then we learn to give thanks for everything fine and great in our
lives. And when we say "Thank you" we are really saying, "This
I am not; I received it as a gift."

I learned something about this during the time when the bombs
were falling. Previously, when I came into my study where all my
books are gathered, I used to think, "All this is my scholarship and
my wisdom, it all belongs to me; it is, so to speak, my extended
self." But when the bombs came and all around us the houses
collapsed I began to think differently: "You can't take it so for
granted that all this belongs to you. It can all be taken away from
you; it has only been given and entrusted to you." So I found myself giving thanks for every day I could still have my treasures.

And so it is with other things too. The things we have—our
family, our friends, our health, the sight of the sea and the
mountains—these things cease to be taken for granted. They
become undeserved gifts when we have learned to thank God
for them. And that gives us a new, a happy attitude toward life.
We learn, as it were, to live more consciously. In every moment

we learn afresh that we are being guided by a loving hand and blessed by a fatherly heart. We stop plodding along and vegetating in monotonous dullness; suddenly we know what living means. We live by virtue of a miracle, and the miracle is this: We are "gifted" people, a tremendous gift has been bestowed upon us. We have a home in this world and the world to come. We no longer have to make any pretensions to ourselves and others. We can come just as we are. Life is worth living, for our life has meaning.

℁ 18 ℞

How to Love Your Neighbor

The Christian message tells us that when love, total devotion to others, is interpreted as a *commandment*, as merely a *duty*, it becomes nothing more than a compulsion and then it has more to do with the nervous system than with the heart. This is the theme I should like to discuss with you today.

First, the question: Why is it that love cannot be a matter of command? Immanuel Kant said over and over again in his ethics that the ethical quality of our conduct is dependent upon the degree to which we have had to conquer ourselves. What he meant was that the ethical always consists in a "thou shalt," and that when it is too easy for us to measure up to this "thou shalt" we have only been obeying our own impulse and thus living unethically. Schiller once poked fun at Kant for this and asked where this Kantian idea of self-conquest would land us. Schiller said, "I dearly love my friends, but, unfortunately, I do so only because I feel so inclined; it vexes me that I am not ethical." What he is saying is that good old Kant could never understand the love of friends as an ethical quality, because one loves friends spontaneously and therefore one does *not* have to overcome oneself to do so. Hence for Kant duty always has in it the element of self-conquest. But this means—and this is why I mention it— that for Kant the ethical also manifests the divided man. On the one hand, man is one who is obedient to an ethical demand, but, on the other hand, he is at the same time the opponent of this demand; he is the man who wants to cultivate his own personality and pursue his inclinations, urges, impulses, who wants to be "himself." So here man is always bipartite. This is actually the case, for every "thou shalt," every act, every command not only gains the man but at the same time brings out the opponent in him. Paul dealt with this in the seventh chapter of Romans.

Therefore love cannot be commanded and this is actually the reason why this is so. For love is always something that possesses my whole heart; love is the whole bent of our heart. When I impose upon myself the "duty" of liking someone because my Christian or pastoral profession demands it of me, this is an intolerable situation not only for myself, but also for the victim of this kind of forced love. People quite naturally take notice that this is an "ethical act" which is merely being put on.

But if this is so, if I cannot command love, how can I get to the place where I love a person in the genuine sense, where the other person really becomes my neighbor?

I want to try as a Christian, now that we have indicated the problem of love in the example from Kant, to set forth a few thoughts that may help us to deal with this question. May I do this by taking an extreme example, the example of loving one's enemy, which is certainly a few degrees more problematical than that of loving one's neighbor?

When the New Testament says that we should love our enemy, does not this mean something other than my pumping up some feelings of love in a situation where all natural, instinctive life demands of me only a defensive reaction? Does not this put me in the very realm of hypocrisy and forced love?

Here is an anecdote. In one of the newer apartment houses which are so flimsy that everything can be heard, there is a row going on because one of the tenants always has his radio on at top volume. In the apartment house there lived an old, wise, very philanthropically minded man who talked to one of the more exasperated tenants in the attempt to calm him down. After a long discussion he told him as a last resort how to get along with radio-neighbors in such a situation: "Yes, you really have to love people in order to put up with them." "You mean to say," said the other, "that I should love a fellow who turns on jazz music at full volume every night at twelve o'clock?" Whereupon the old man replied, "Well, it's no trick at all to love someone who has no radio."

Behind the humor of this little story I ask you not to overlook the deeper problem posed by this brief dialogue. Is love a kind of trick that one must learn and practice upon an enemy, a radio-neighbor? Is this really a matter of methods and exercises? We may attempt to answer this with another anecdote, and then try to bring out the thought that is behind it. In Remarque's book about World War I, *All Quiet on the Western Front*, we find the following scene. The author describes an assault in which at one point, when they come in contact with the enemy, he leaped into a shell hole. In the shell hole he found an Englishman. After the first shock of fright he considered what he should do now. Should they proceed to bayonet each other? But this bit of reflection was soon ended when he saw that the other man was severely wounded, so badly wounded that the German soldier was humanly touched by his condition. He gave him a drink from his canteen and the man gave him a look of gratitude. The Englishman then indicated that he wanted him to open his breast pocket. He did so and an envelope containing pictures of the man's family fell out. He obviously wanted to look at them once more. In that moment before the English soldier died, the German held up before him the pictures of his wife, his children, and his mother.

So much for the scene. Here we have something remarkable manifesting itself, something that goes to the depths of anthropology. Here the attacker suddenly suffers a complete change in his way of seeing things. At first, that is, in the moment of battle, the other man was for him only the wearer of a uniform. That is, he was only the representative of a collective, an element in a hostile front, an enemy. But the moment he came upon this wounded, defenseless man in the shell hole and then also saw him in connection with the pictures of his family, he realized that the other man with whom he has to deal—including the man with the radio—is never *merely* the man with the enemy's uniform or the annoying instrument, but that he also lives in another, completely different, dimension, that he is loved by his wife, his children, his parents, and that he himself loves. These are two totally different dimensions.

And when we realize these two dimensions in which a man lives, we begin to understand one of the mysteries in the New Testament record, namely, that Jesus Christ on the cross was able to say concerning his executioners, "Father, forgive them; for they know not what they do." What happened here was this transformation in one's way of seeing. What these words of the Crucified make clear is that loving one's enemy is not an extreme effort of will in which he fought down all the feelings of hatred within him, but rather that it was this transformed way of seeing. In other words, he no longer saw the people around him, these people who were hateful and malicious, merely as representatives of a hostile front; he saw them as the lost children of his Father who were intended to be something totally different in life and who had simply fallen away from what God really meant their lives to be and had become lost on the wrong road. Because he was able to love his enemies, Christ saw in the other person— even the persons who were very critical and threatening to his life—the original intent, the original design of his Father in heaven; he saw through the layer of dirt that covered the life, the original lineaments of the other person.

This then raises the question: "Who is, what is the other person who should be my neighbor?" I should say that this is the fundamental question of our Christian calling.

And who the other person really is I may again seek to show by means of an example. You know the story of the Prodigal

Son. If one were to say who and what the Prodigal Son was, where the focal point of his existence lay, one would have to say that this lost son was a bad egg who squandered his goods and his health with harlots and other riffraff. Or would we not have to say, "No, the lost son is one who is being sought by his father despite all his confusions." *This* is his mystery!

Therefore we never grasp the mystery of a person when we merely photograph him, as it were, in every possible shocking situation and then say: "*This* is what he is, this is his phenotype." No, the Christian sees his genotype, sees him in his uniqueness, sees him as he was meant to be.

Only as we realize how Christ looked upon men, seeing through the covering layer to the original man beneath, will we begin to understand many things about him which we would not otherwise understand. He is the one to whom all power has been given in heaven and on earth; he has a cosmic reference, he is the ruler of the world. But strangely enough, it now appears that this King who encompasses the whole world in his realm has time to stop and talk to the *individual*. For us men, who are always thinking in strategic, economic, propagandistic terms, this is one of those astonishing things which are simply incomprehensible. That Jesus Christ does not go directly to the "upper ten thousand," to the big cities, that he does not occupy the strategic key positions, but that he stops and talks to a poor woman, a blind man, a leper—in any case, to those who are outside the pale of society and have no productive sociological value whatsoever—this is incomprehensible. We can understand this only if we see that this other, individual person is infinitely valuable.

We simply must allow ourselves to be reminded of this because it is in this valuation that we, who are inclined not only to mechanize but also to make a "thing" of man, will begin to realize the whole difference between our world and the world of Jesus. It is a grave sign that everywhere in life today we hear terms used which make a "thing" of man—the physicians speak of "cases," the military speak of "manpower," the schools speak of "teaching-force." Without attaching too much significance to this terminology, I ask whether our weariness of people, the fact that we feel our neighborly love to be a drudgery, does not stem from the fact that we no longer see this other dimension in people, that for us they have actually become "cases," depersonalized objects whom we simply manipulate.

The important point is that we must change our way of looking at our neighbor, not that we must stimulate and animate our will to be humanitarian. We must change our eyes, not our will. But this brings us right back to the same problem that has been literally dogging us all along, since everything depends upon this *one* question: ultimately I can no more put on new eyes upon command than I can love upon command. They must be given to me. Nevertheless there are some things I can do in order that they may be given to me. Allow me to point again to a New Testament story in which this problem of being given something becomes clear. It is the parable of the Unmerciful Servant.

The parable deals with a king who forgives one of his subjects a tremendous debt. The man had cheated the king. He embezzled funds running into many millions, which he could never repay, so that, according to the custom of the time, there was nothing left but to give up himself and his family to be sold into slavery. Utterly shattered he came to his superior, confessed what he had done, and begged forgiveness. It was granted to him; the bond was torn up and he went scot-free. No sooner had he returned home when one of his own servants came to him and told him that such and such had happened to him and he had put his hand into the cashbox and some coins had stuck to it (a sum that was tiny compared with what his employer had taken from his king). And forthwith the man took the legal point of view and had his servant thrown into prison until he paid it all back. The parable closes with a very somber prognosis for those who act likewise, those who regard people only from the legal point of view.

And this means that here again we are summoned to meet the people around us, who may owe us something or who get on our nerves, not by making an effort of will or self-control; we are simply shown that we should stop and remember what has been

forgiven *us*. God does not interest himself in us, he does not accept us because we have such beautiful blue eyes, because we are
"men" (*homines sapientes!*), because it would pay him to establish a kingdom of God for our sake. Such men might sooner be
answered with a statement made by Nietzsche, who once described men as "vermin on the crust of the earth." And the
Psalmist said, "What is man that thou art mindful of him?"
Nothing! Here it is emphatically pointed out that we men are
something only because God has bestowed his heart upon us. God
loves us, not because we are so valuable; rather we are valuable
because God loves us. This is the miracle by which we live. And
now this parable does nothing else but give us a command—
and remember now that this is a real command—to be obeyed in
these critical situations in our lives in which we owe something
to people. It commands us to turn our eyes to those facts to
which we owe all we have and are: we have nothing else to pass
on to others except that which we have received. I would say
that this again is a kind of antithesis of the Gospel to much that
comes to us from human moral teaching, of which Kant was perhaps the greatest representative. Is it really true that everything
begins with the command "Thou shalt"? Or must it not rather
begin with our first being given something? The Gospel says to
us: You cannot give anything whatsoever to your neighbor except that which you have received. No man can give more than
he has; first something is given to you. And the real secret of our
life is to remember this first thing which we have received and
to learn the art of keeping in contact with our neighbor at the
critical moments and passing on to him what we have received.

This brings us to two concluding thoughts. In the first place,
in all that we have considered here we have quite naturally come
up against the question of how natural love and Christian love
are related to each other. I would say that the natural love which
we know as human beings (that is, the whole realm of sympathy
and antipathy, the realm of Eros, and also the honorable realm of
humanitarian duty toward others) is related to "loveworthiness."
We naturally love someone who is "loveworthy," as our language

expresses it, and we trust someone who is "trustworthy." But if we go back and take another look at how Jesus Christ treated people, and see him loving the publicans and the harlots, for example, then we see something happening which is totally different, something which simply cannot be subsumed under this concept of natural love which we have just described. What happens here is a creative act by which Christ penetrates what I have called the layer of dirt and sees the original man. But when that happens to a person, when a man or the Son of Man, as here, looks upon him according to what he was really meant to be, then something altogether remarkable happens. Perhaps it can be compared with what happens in photography. The real image of him comes out as the development brings out the hidden image on a piece of film. So it was that people whom Christ had looked upon and loved went away different from what they were before; the original image was "loved out" of them.

This love of Christ is creative; it ventures even with the wicked and the soiled and draws out the real image within. I once tried to emulate this, though the analogy is extremely poor. I was directing an organization in which one of the members was a somewhat doubtful character whom the others did not care for. He was, in fact, not exactly stable or serious. Out of all the rest I chose this young man to be the treasurer. The others were amazed, to say the least, that I should have made such a choice. But I was actually trying for once to act in accord with what we have just been talking about. But then something quite remarkable happened—though naturally this is not intended to be taken as a prescription for general financial policy—the young man *became* trustworthy! It was therefore just the opposite of what occurs in the normal causal nexus: it was not the given trustworthiness of the other person that provoked my trust, but rather my trust that provoked trustworthiness in the other person. The secret of what is called "love" in the New Testament is that it sees the other person in his original state (in that dimension which the German soldier saw in the shell hole) and that in this way it acquires a creative character. Many a person with whom we come in contact, who grates on us and is so emphatically unlovable, is probably that way because we have not loved him enough, because we have not yet practiced upon him the function of the photographic developer.

When in normal life we love other people we always interpret this as a kind of recompense for the other person's lovableness. He deserves to be loved because he is so charming, because he has a decent character; so I recompense him with my love. I have exaggerated this a bit, but generally this is the way we feel. But here we are told something completely different: we are rewarded for loving the other person, for seeing him in this other dimension, by the fact that he becomes "loveworthy."

What, then, is the secret of the other person, my neighbor? This I can answer only as a Christian—and I say this explicitly, not only to put our cards on the table, but because I believe that a merely humanistic or humanitarian answer will actually get you into trouble. This is the point at which I really believe that the ultimate decisions are made!

There is a story that has been told concerning Josef Stalin which has profound implications and should help us with our problem. Stalin was once addressing a rally of raftsmen. On this occasion it turned out that one horse and one man were missing. The people raised a furious fuss about the horse. The loss of a man troubled them not at all, for they said: "We can get or breed all the men we want." Whereupon Stalin delivered a little speech which was so impressive to many who read it in the newspapers at the time that for a moment they forgot the bugbear of Bolshevism. He said, "It is a terrible thing that you are more excited about the horse than about the man. Just stop and consider that it is the *man* who controls the machines and that the development of our technology will do us no good whatsoever if we do not have first-class skilled workers. The man is the main thing in the apparatus."

I should say that it is always a suspicious thing to hear such "humanistic" utterances coming from such a source. Why? The answer to that question will at the same time be the answer to our last question.

When Stalin made this statement to the raftsmen he was in reality *not* revering the human being at all. In this statement of his there is no recognition that man has a soul or an eternal destiny or that he exists for eternal salvation or condemnation. For Stalin in this rather emotional appeal man is simply elevated to a higher rank within the hierarchy of technological means. He is not set over against the technical world as a human being with the prerogatives and the infinite worth of his human soul, but merely designated as the most valuable factor, the key figure within the technological enterprise.

In other words, one can see the other person, the neighbor with whom we have to deal as ministers, politicians, or nurses, from two fundamentally different points of view. One can *either* value him as Jesus Christ does, and a Christian in emulation of him does —namely, by recognizing the infinite value of the human soul, knowing what God has expended upon him, acknowledging that he has been dearly purchased and that he is the apple of God's eye—we could go on mentioning many other expressions that convey the infinite value of the human being. That is one point of view. Or we can value him because of his "utility," because of his capacity for performing a function in the technological or production process or in economic life.

These are, therefore, the two ultimate criteria which I have for assessing the nature, the essential nature of my fellow man: either his infinite value or his utility. To characterize them more precisely, the utility of man always relates to his immanent value, to what he possesses in the way of capacities, strength, working-power, talents, whereas the infinite value of which the Bible speaks is always a value which is not his own. The very expressions which we have just used showed this: man is dearly purchased, he is loved. He acquires his value by reason of something that happens to him from the outside; something that someone else does for him.

I once saw an illustration of this thought of "alien" dignity when I was in the first form in school. We had there a boy whom we simply could not stand because he was a pusher. And as is typical at that age we were cooking up a plot to give him a thrashing in order to take him down a bit. About the time when this was to take place, I saw his father, who was probably the most distinguished man in our town, one to whom we all looked up, bringing him to school. I saw how he let him off at the gate of the school, put his hand on his head, patted his cheek, and kept waving to him when they parted. It was strange how suddenly this boy was changed in my eyes. True, he was still the same pusher we knew, still the same somewhat sloppy fellow, but this boy was loved by this man. This gave him in my eyes something like an "alien dignity," not an immanent quality of character or anything else; but this splendor of another's love lay around him.

We must decide between these two images of man, for this decision constitutes the real help that we may give in every critical human situation. When another person gets on my nerves, when I can no longer see the human being in him, but only a glitter of hatred for me or an unsavory hulk, I must remember that he is one who was once designed to be something, one who was loved.

This was why Bodelschwingh could offer such passionate resistance when Hitler's orders demanded the removal of his epileptics and feeble-minded from Bethel. But the question of whether these people were to be disposed of also depends upon this decision, and it shows us that this decision is important, not only for nurses, doctors, and Christians in general. For anybody who takes the position that man does not have this "alien dignity," that the secret of his existence does not rest upon the fact that he has been dearly purchased, but rather that the worth of man depends upon his utility, must necessarily come to the point where he asks: "Is this man still worth anything? Is an epileptic, a mentally ill person, an idiot, a total cripple still utilizable?" And if he is not utilizable, he must be liquidated, he must be scrapped just because he is useless material. Many a prisoner from

Russia has told us how men there were evaluated merely on the basis of the potential ability to work and, in order not to talk only about others, we have experienced this ourselves under the former regime. I would venture to assert that all the cruelties that have occurred and still occur in the world are not the result of a criminal strain in those who do such things. These persons may even be idealists. Whether they do such things or whether man is sacroscanct to them depends upon the first principle of our anthropology; it depends upon the question whether man is merely utilizable or whether he has infinite worth, and thus security. If he has this, he is under the protection of an eternal goodness. Everything depends upon that.

❧ 19 ❧

What Does It Mean to Trust?

In what follows I should like to share with you parts of a letter which I wrote to a young soldier during the war. He had gone through many terrible experiences, and slowly but surely the mask of hideous cruelty slipped over the face of the Father in whom he had hitherto believed. He was beset by the question, "How can God permit this to happen?" and we corresponded about this. An excerpt from one of my letters reads as follows:

"Do you remember Faust's experience on Easter eve when he had already put the poisoned cup to his lips and was terrified by the doubt and desperation that rose up in his heart? Just then he heard the sound of the Easter bells, and the sound of them came to him like a message of deliverance, like the voice of a brother laying his hand on his shoulder and saying: You must not die, for, after all, God has opened the heavens.

"What Faust experienced there in a dim, remote parabolical way comes to Christians as the living voice of God, a voice that does not come miraculously from the clouds, it is true, but which is embedded in the words of a brother man who has been privileged to say to me in God's stead, 'I have called you by name, you are mine,' a man who comes to me and puts my hand in the hand of God. At such times it becomes clearer than at others that God's Word is not something that comes from the dim past, not a pious tradition with the odor of antiquity about it, but that it is spoken *here and now,* that our brother has just received it from heaven, and that the voice of the Lord himself is still trembling within it.

"Perhaps we can grasp this Word which is spoken *now* and to *me* only if we go back and think about the miracle of Christmas. Just as God became man in the mystery of Holy Night, so his Word is constantly coming down and repeatedly becoming the word of man, and this 'brother in Christ' bears it in his hand and on his lips and I receive it and allow it to be spoken to me, just as Zacharias took the Child Jesus in his arms and actually held the heavenly blessing in his hands.

" 'This we must realize in death, in the depths, and in doubt,' said Luther. 'I have this Word that I *shall* live, no matter how terribly death crowds in upon me.' Take hold of that, my dear friend, I *have* the Word, I hold it in my hands, it is being spoken to me now! And therefore I need not and I cannot go on saying, 'I once heard something about such a Word; it seems to me that there might be such a thing.' No, I *have* the Word, I hear it now.

"It speaks to me so personally that it says 'thou' and it does not merely speak in general terms about the destiny of mankind as philosophical systems do. No, this Word says to me, 'You shall live, you, very you!' But even that is perhaps too weakly and inadequately expressed. It is not an 'it' that speaks to me, but rather a brother, and through him God himself. And now I can say, as Luther did, 'Death, death be hanged, the Lord has promised me that I shall live. This I believe!'

"Whenever I read this saying of Luther, with its concluding 'This I believe,' flung down like a defiant period at the end of a sentence, it sounds to me almost like a decision: 'That's final; now God has the responsibility for what he has said—even for my faith. For everything else grows hazy and blurred, especially my pious resolutions. The one thing that stands secure and solid is this promise: *You shall live*. I stake everything on this card. God declares that he has it in his hand. So he has the responsibility. In his name I cast myself into the night and hope that I shall fall into the hands of God.'

"That's what Luther's concluding words, 'This I believe,' sound like. We might also say that they look like a signature dashed down with such defiance that the ink spurted. But if this is a signature, then it is only a countersignature, a mark of avowal written with tremendous nerve and blindfolded eyes, accepting God's promise that I shall live which he has signed and sealed with his blood.

"Dear friend, do you remember what you wrote in your first letter about your closing your eyes and playing dead like an animal? You were referring then to the shells bursting around you and the moments of extreme danger, and you said that this was not cowardice or merely sticking one's head in the sand. But you must see that *faith* too has such moments—moments when it shuts its eyes and lets itself fall, moments when it knows that now it's either the abyss or the hand of God, when it dares to take the leap solely because God has said the Word, knowing, despite everything to the contrary, that it can end, not in the abyss, but only in the hands of God.

"Do not misunderstand me, my dear K. It is by no means true that we must blind ourselves in order to be able to believe. On the contrary, we must understand that faith goes along with the greatest clearheadedness ever revealed to us men—the clearheadedness and the realism of the men of the Bible. It is as if faith *arms* and sharpens our eyes, as if it teaches us to see things in and around and above ourselves that are closed to the natural function of our eyes. But as if to remind us that it is not the light of this eye itself that shines here, but rather that it is a borrowed light, a light in which the thoughts of God himself shine (Ps. 36:9), it is as if to remind us of this fact, I say, that our own eyes must repeatedly grow dim and die, experiencing the truth which every Christian knows, that one must die in order to live. We have the promise that as Christians we shall become clear-sighted men who are permitted to know the secrets of God. But this clear-sightedness is born only of eyes that renounce themselves; it is born in those who dare to believe *blindly*, because they know that, watching over them, are eyes that have no pleasure in the proud eyes of man who measures God's governance of the world by his own parish-pump politics and presumes to sit upon his throne.

"You see, my friend, that because all this is so and because our eyes are at bottom domineering eyes, eyes that are opposed to God, their light must die if they are to see the light of God. Therefore they must always go through 'blind' faith. It would appear to me, however, that those who had been blind before and then received their sight from Jesus saw *more* of his glory than did all the good, critical, hawk-eyed observers put together. It is true, of course, that even those whose eyes had been opened by God could not see all the mysteries of the Christ. It may be that only a short time later they were terrified by what they saw happen on Golgotha. It may be that even they began to ask in dull despair: 'How can God permit such a thing to happen?' Perhaps, perhaps! For even lightened eyes are not yet 'seeing' eyes. No, they belong to men who 'walk by faith, *not* by sight' (II Cor. 5:7); they belong to men who trust the 'higher thoughts' that God is thinking far above them; they belong to men who day by day bury their prayers and their understanding in the will of God, despite the protests of soul and mind and reason. That, and that alone, is trust. That's what faith means.

"It has grown late now, my friend, and I have stepped out on the veranda to breathe some fresh air. Below me lies the lightless, darkened plain of the Rhine. Many a soldier has united himself with those he loved at home by looking at the stars at night, in order that their paths of vision might meet in the distance. Perhaps you too are looking up at this very moment.

"But I still cannot see anything. The heavens are black and dark, though I know there are no clouds. The glare of my desk lamp is still in my eyes. And we never see the firmament as long as human lights dominate our eyes. Another moment and these lights will have died; then the stars will be visible. First the bright ones and then the distant ones, in space far beyond my comprehension. Then at length the glory of the firmament will open out above me and I will know that even then there are many stars and spaces which I cannot see. But they are all under the same heaven and there are eyes that have numbered them all, eyes that know them all."

❧ 20 ☙

Faith and the Philosophies*

Philosophies are always in danger of taking a creaturely entity, like the mind, or *bios* (the Greek word for "life"), or economics, and elevating it to the rank of God.

The consequence of such a reversing of Creator and creature is always a profound disorder—indeed, a breakdown—of the world; for the creaturely entity which is elevated to the dignity of God is never equal to the task and is simply incapable of embracing and governing the totality of life.

Suppose, for example, that we make an absolute of that created thing which is called "mind" or "spirit" or "intellect" and elevate it to the rank of *the* principle of the world. When this is done it cannot fail to produce a certain intellectualism, a view in which the intellect is the supreme value, which is incapable of controlling the deep undercurrents and irrational forces in human life. It is therefore no wonder when the forces of blood and instinct rebel against an intellectualistic philosophy and the vital gods demand their place at the hearth. The whole world of instinct and primi-

*Here and throughout *Weltanschaung* (world-view) is translated as "philosophy," "philosophy of life" or "view of the world." (Trans.)

tive feeling thrusts for release and development and feels that it is not understood and is not bound by the authority of the intellect. It feels that it has been left out of account and therefore its drive is toward rebellion. This is the only explanation of Friedrich Nietzsche's revolution, for example. Nietzsche's thought is a single concentrated outcry against the rule of the abstract, intellectual mind. In him spoke man's tormented blood which had been subjugated to an alien master and, as it were, ignored. Friedrich Nietzsche was a kind of escape valve which gave vent to the untamed forces of blood and instinct.

But we sense that this attempt to proclaim *life* as the ultimate principle of the world is also incapable of embracing the whole. That is to say, a purely biological view of the world leans over on the other side and leaves the mind and the spirit unsatisfied. The mind is *more* and it also *wants* to be more than a mere irradiation, a mere reflex of the *bios*-organism. Gothe's *Faust* and Bach's *St. Matthew Passion* are meant to be taken as struggles for ultimate truth, not simply as products exuded by natural biological processes. Moreover, the purely biological view of life does not do justice to the fact that man is more than a mere organism, that he is an ethical person, the image of God, and that he possesses an infinite value even when in the biological sense he is called old and useless or sick and unfit to live, and fails to meet the ideal of perfect natural health.

So it is inevitable that these forces of the spirit and the ethical should rebel against the assaults of a purely biological view.

Similar reactions can be shown in all the attempts to base a view of the world upon a created entity. For example, when the *individual* is deified and philosophy proclaims nothing but the so-called "right of personality" to develop in accord with its own nature, then the *community* is very likely to feel that it is being left out of account and begins to protest against "individualism."

On the other hand, when the *community* is deified and there arises a philosophy of collectivism, which subordinates the individual to the whole in a way that extinguishes the personality, then the individual personality feels that it is being ignored and tyrannized over and proceeds to rebel again in favor of a new individualism. If all the signs are not deceiving, we are now in a new phase of development of this latter kind. Young people who have lived in barracks for years or have been regimented in other ways are violently insisting upon an individual, private life which is subject only to their own control.

I have mentioned these facts for one reason only and that is that this terrible crisis in the history of views of the world can be understood only from the point of view of the Bible, that is to say, from the point of view of faith in a Creator and the First Commandment. We can state it this way: When men use their philosophies to elevate a creaturely entity to the level of the ultimate meaning of the world and thus put it in the place of the Creator, they deliver the world over to its downfall. For we have seen that each of these creaturely entities always leaves whole areas of life untouched and ungoverned and thus delivers them over to revolt. The creaturely entity "community" drives the individual to rebellion; the creaturely entity "individual" touches off the revolt of the forces of community. So it has been and so it is in every philosophy you can think of.

Has not this been the reason why the history of Western civilization with its increasing secularization has become a veritable chain of rebellions?

If we trace the course of the inner history of our continent in the last several centuries, our heads are likely to spin, so rapid has been the succession of philosophical slogans and watchwords, so quickly have they toppled whatever gods that happened to be enthroned. It has been a veritable parade of idols, and as they pass by, how comical these gods look from behind! Ideas that were taken in deadly seriousness a few decades ago now strike us as vapid and ludicrous. How the philosophies, the gods have succeeded one another! One recognizes them by their suffixes; they always end in "ism." It would be much too confusing to enumerate them all as they have succeeded one another: nationalism, sensualism, idealism, materialism, nomism, biologism, bolshevism, and so on and on.

When we see this mad parade of gods passing by we are reminded of three fundamental laws of the Bible which here prove
their validity in graphic fashion:

1. Whenever God the Creator is deposed as the absolute and
sovereign Lord of the world and our life, the *gods take over.*

2. But whenever the false gods are enthroned, there is always
conflict between the gods, and this means a battle of philosophies
of life and therefore the threat of chaos. What this means in con-
crete terms is all too clear to us in an age of nationalistic philosophies. We have seen this philosophy take hold of nations all
over the world and become a new form of polytheism among
the individual nations. The nations had their own gods and then
proceeded to make themselves the supreme standard for the
world. This is what gave to the last world war its apocalyptic
character; the national gods battled each other, as it were, in
the air above the nations. A really Trojan situation! And therefore mutual understanding also disappeared from the world because the binding force which is God was gone and the nations
with their own gods, that is, with their own absolutized minds,
fought each other. So there is no human arm that can call a halt
to this conflict of gods.

3. Finally, whenever God is deposed and the false gods are
worshiped, the result is always a *twilight of the gods;* that is, the
absolutized, deified creaturely entity immediately proves its in-
ability to bind together broad areas of life and is therefore able
to maintain itself only for a brief time. The result is an increasing
and more rapid attrition of these philosophies.

Then there is one last thing that becomes clear, and that is
that there is no human possibility of stopping this development
and calling a halt to this parade and conflict of gods. That is to say,
it is a characteristic of gods that men can indeed help them to
seize the throne, but that at the very moment of their accession
to the throne they take command, and then no human arm can
topple them. Only new gods can overthrow the old gods, only
to see their thrones challenged immediately by coming wielders
of power. Moreover, from the very first day, the countenances

of the new gods are clouded by the twilight, the shadows of which, by eternal, immutable laws, keep reaching out to seize them. A touch of sadness lies upon the faces of all the gods, and a melancholy knowledge of their own transiency drives them to haste and a dangerous overextension of their dominion. They know that their "time is short" (Rev. 12:12).

Everything that we have been compelled to say about this conflict of the gods and the philosophies, about this profound disorder of our modern world, has not been said merely to be negative and to paint the picture as black as can be. It is true, of course, that what we are dealing with here is "apostasy." (This is actually the key word with which to unlock the inner history of Western civilization.) But we have been able to arrive at this conclusion only in the name of a positive fact—the fact that there *is* a Creator who is the Lord of heaven and earth and that Christ stands at the beginning and the end of history. And this means that we are not wandering about in a hopeless maze at the mercy of the dark and enigmatic powers of fate, but rather that we are merely fleeing from a Lord who is waiting for us.

The Gospel tells us of the *kairos*, the "acceptable time," the "today" in which we may hearken to his voice. To hear the Gospel means to be assured of a new beginning. To receive forgiveness means to receive a new future. The Gospel knows that there is a "new creation" because it knows the One who creates. History is not left to operate according to its own autonomy, its own laws, nor is it subject to the law of rise and fall that rules the gods. No, it rests in hands that are seeking and searching for men. The ultimate impulses of history issue from a *heart*. And the threat of the end is only *one* of its alternatives. The *other* alternative is to come back home.

✺ 21 ✺

On Being Afraid of Life

Some time ago, using the familiar Gallup procedure, a number of questions were addressed to young people, particularly students. One of these questions was: "What is the basic feeling you have toward life?" Sixty per cent of them replied with a shocking unanimity: fear. Why is it that persons who do not by any means impress one as being anxious or depressed should give such a strange answer?

If one wishes to ascertain whether a person is afraid or anxious, one would be inclined to explore what his attitude is toward death. But when one attempts to test the correctness of this poll by this means, one very soon finds that there is a hitch in it. For one cannot say of our generation that it is unusually fearful of death. Sometimes we have noted with surprise that fearlessness in the face of death is not necessarily brought about by what is called a "religious stay" at all, but that religiously indifferent—indeed, atheistic and nihilistic people—may be quite calm and composed with regard to death.

We probably shall not go wrong if we assume that what is expressed in this Gallup-poll reply is not fear of death but fear of life. If Luther, the medieval monk, was filled with the anxiety of guilt in the presence of the divine Judge and this wrung from his lips the question: "How can I find a gracious God?" then people today are shaken by the anxiety of fate, by fear of the appalling and unfathomable contingencies of life. Where once there stood the judging God there is now a vacuum, an empty place.

Perhaps Christian proclamation and preaching ought to re-think this situation completely and search out man where he actually is, in this abyss where he suffers fear and anxiety. Actually, the Holy Book of Christianity does not merely address man at the point of his sin and guilt, but primarily at the point of his fear and anxiety. Few sentences recur as often as the call to come back to the peace of God which is usually introduced by the words: "Fear not!"

In order to understand the nature of this anxiety it may be well to examine the root meaning of the word. The word "anxiety" derives from the Latin word *angustia* which means shortness of breath, the feeling of constriction which occurs in the maximum state of fear—in connection, for example, with angina pectoris. It is characteristic of the term "anxiety" that it points to a condition in which the thing which makes me afraid is subordinate or does not appear at all. In other words, the nature of anxiety is the undefinable character of the feeling of being threatened.

In order to understand this we may think of the image of the Midgard serpent in Germanic mythology. Beyond the horizon a great serpent encircles the earth and we are all enclosed in this constriction. The whole world is surrounded by something weird and uncanny. The shadow and the terror of this dark "something" weigh upon everything, even the joys and the feasts which we may celebrate in this terribly constricted world. This is the point where the full impact of the terror of anxiety appears. As long as I am merely afraid, that is, as long as I fear something definite, I still have hope also. I fear, for example, that I have cancer, but perhaps it is only a harmless swelling, and perhaps also there may be some unexpected prospect of curing it. I fear that my missing son is dead, but he may perhaps be alive nevertheless. But all this is different in the anguishing toils of the Midgard serpent. There the whole world, including all fears and hopes, is in jeopardy, and hence the shadow of the twilight of the gods bears down upon even the forces of hope. In times of great catastrophe the great serpent tightens, as it were, its coils!

It would be strange if man did not do everything in his power to free himself from this anxiety. How he attempts to do this is forcibly expressed in Ernst Jünger's essay *The Man in the Moon*. "As far as any meaning is concerned—that is, as far as any discernible order in history is concerned—my existence is more hopeless [and therefore productive of anxiety] than any other on earth. As a man on the moon I could never locate meaning anywhere [for, after all, I would find myself in the midst of an icy, cratered, lunar landscape]. Since I have given up thinking about the meaning of my life I get along fairly well." In other words, one attempts to deal with anxiety, not by seeking to wrest a meaning from life in Faustian fashion, but rather by simply ignoring the question of meaning, by living from day to day without asking any questions, by vegetating, as it were.

An outstanding example of this way of dealing with the question of meaning, and thus with anxiety, is the case of the famous Colonel Lawrence, who became world-famous through his role as leader of the Arab revolt, a man whom Churchill called one of the greatest hopes of the British Empire. After his brilliant military exploits in the desert this world-famous colonel enlisted as a common soldier in the ground personnel of the RAF. Why? "I am doing this to serve a purely mechanical purpose, not as a driver but as a shadow of a machine. . . . One of the benefits is to be merely a part of the machine. One teaches oneself that things do not depend upon oneself." Lawrence had performed great deeds; he had assumed great responsibilities for the Arabs, who idolized him. But fundamentally his work had failed and the meaninglessness of all that he had accomplished poured in upon him. The anxiety of life triumphed over this bravest of men. And he tried to free himself of it by turning himself into a machine, by trying to become one small screw in a machine.

Thus man often frees himself from the anxiety of life, from meaninglessness, not by continuing to ask the question of meaning, but by ceasing to ask it—in other words, by ceasing to be a human being. He makes himself anonymous, he allows himself to evaporate in the mass, or he becomes merely an organ that carries out certain functions and processes whose purposes and goals no longer concern him. Here he may find peace. But it is the delusive peace of a technological Nirvana, the peace of self-renunciation, flight into superficiality. And all of this confronts us with overwhelming force in our present-day way of life. There are few manifestations of modern life which do not bear the mark of this anxiety of life and flight from it.

This presents us with the question whether there is a genuine way of overcoming this anxiety instead of this delusive way of evading it.

The Christian cannot speak of overcoming this anxiety without thinking of him who said, "In the world you have tribulation [anxiety]; but be of good cheer, I have overcome the world." Now, the surprising thing in the biblical message is this: it finds the opposite of fear and anxiety in love. "There is no fear"— one could just as well translate "anxiety"—"in love," says the First Letter of John. This is surprising because here we do not find (as one would expect) moral will power, fortitude, and heroism played off against anxiety. These, after all, are merely repressed anxiety, not anxiety overcome. The positive power that overcomes anxiety is love. And we shall understand what is meant by this only if we understand what anxiety is at its deepest root, namely, that anxiety is a broken tie, a disturbed relationship, and that love is a restored relationship. The person who sees the phenomenon which is Christ, and thus realizes that the foundation of this world is fatherly and that he is loved, that person loses his anxiety. He loses it not because the menacing, constricting forces are gone; in Dürer's picture, "Knight, Death and the

Devil," they are all there, still lurking on the knight's road. But they no longer have any power over him. If we were to put it in parable form, we might say: "When I walk with my hand in the Father's, when I am sure of his hand, then I have no fear, no anxiety, even in the darkest forest."

Even Christ himself faced the anguishing riddles of life, and according to the oldest account, the last word he uttered on the cross was: "My God, my God, why hast thou forsaken me?" But the significant thing is that he did not shout this cry of dereliction into the darkness of Golgotha which was swallowing him up in its meaninglessness, but rather he was addressing his Father, "My God . . . ," in other words, he was still holding fast to the Father's hand. He brought his anxiety to the Father, and he put it there once and for all.

He who is anxious and knows Christ may be assured that he is not alone in his anxiety, but that Christ, too, has gone through it. And this means a completely new attitude toward the future; no longer is the future a befogged landscape into which I peer anxiously because all kinds of obscure perils are brewing there for me. No, everything is changed: we do not know what is coming, but we know *who* is coming. And he who possesses the last hour no longer needs to fear the next minute.

❧ 22 ❧

Is Technology Diabolical?

Technology is by no means a mere continuation of the development of the old "familiar" craftsmanship. A look at a modern assembly line, let alone modern methods of automation, reveals to us a totally different and unfamiliar world, which at essential points is discontinuous with earlier periods of history. Manual workers' tools are amenable to human hands and we have a relation of immediacy to what is fashioned in this way. In technology, however, through the interposition of natural forces such as steam, electricity, and atomic power, there has arisen a qualitatively *new* world of production which no longer lies in the hands of men, but within which man is becoming more and more a functionary.

What we have called the interposition of natural forces brings with it a relationship of mediacy to that which is produced with the aid of natural forces. And it is precisely this intermediate area which then begins to generate its *own* processes. It begins, as it were, to make history and to outrun the men who thought they were making technological history. Man's immediacy and freedom of action diminishes, as it were, to the one instant in which he exercises the initiative in starting these processes and in the next instant these processes themselves become autonomous and lead us where we do not wish to go.

It was doubtless this observation that compelled the invention of that somewhat "mythical" phrase "the revolt of the means" and thus assigned to these intermediate forces a dignity that made them bearers of leading roles in the drama of history. For to at least the same degree that man occupies himself with technological progress and the refinement of technical methods of fabrication, he is also beginning to reflect upon how he can *assert himself* against this technology which he has conjured up and which is now assuming the role of a fellow protagonist or even an antagonist. It was in line with this that Nicholas Berdyaev once said that in our technological world utopias seem to us to be far more realizable than was formerly believed to be possible. But now we are confronted with the altogether different question of how we can escape its ultimate realization. We are beginning to strive for a non-utopian, a less perfect world. Thus one might say that we are trying to leap from a train which is carrying us down the steep track of this intermediate area to an unwanted, oppressive (!) perfection.

In this connection we must not confine our thinking only to atomic power and technology which is determined by the *physical* sciences; we must also think of the technology which is determined by the *biological* sciences. Once we pursue the idea that all things can be "made," including man himself, it turns out, paradoxically, that man is the one who ends up being "made." This secular, physical realm reluctantly but unmistakably opens up metaphysical vistas.

But we do not have to go to the borderline situations to find illustrative cases. Plain everyday life confronts us with the same problems. To mention one example, we not only "use" the telephone, but we are also afraid of it, because it uses us, because it interrupts the organic course of our work or our rest, and because in angry moments we are therefore inclined to class it with the appointment book and the internal revenue office in the triumvirate of a modern dictatorship. So, who dictates to whom? Is it the bell or the receiver that dictates to me or is it I who dictate into the microphone? Thus technology becomes an intrusion into our life of something alien that lays its spell upon us and as a manifestation of a new omnipotent force can take on an almost religious significance. In a strange imitation of the real thing these phenomena seem to emanate veneration, fascination, and fear. In the history of thought this alien character of technology can be best illustrated by reference to the Hegelian-Marxist concept of the transformation of quantity into quality: technology is not merely the quantitative summation of scientific knowledge and mechanical skills, but rather, as this summation emerges, something essentially new comes into being, namely, the totally different thing which is technology itself.

It is the biologists especially who have called our attention to this highly remarkable fact that technology has come upon us as a kind of alien invasion, a fact which perhaps has been least noticed by the technologists themselves. Konrad Lorenz, for example, in his profound books about animals, has pointed out that in earlier periods of man's history the great climatic and geological changes in environment took place very slowly and that therefore man had correspondingly long periods in which to adjust himself to the changed environmental conditions. Now technology is likewise producing sudden changes in our environmental conditions. And they are plain to be seen. These changes produced by technology differ, however, from the processes induced by geological and climatic changes in that they have come upon us *suddenly*. They have occurred within a few decades, and the picture of our grandfathers suddenly returning from the grave and trying to cross one of our main streets would be an illustration of the speed of this development. Innumerable problems in our modern technicized culture, all the way from traffic conditions to statesmanship, are certainly to be traced back essentially to the fact that we have not acclimated ourselves to these radically changed conditions and that we are moving about incautiously, shiveringly, and often terrifiedly in this new atomic world.

It is obvious that man's creative capacity always (and particularly in the area of technics) consists not only in the power of construction but also of destruction, a fact which Goethe expressed symbolically by having Mephistopheles accompany the creative Faust, indicating that a demonic power is inherent in all Faustian-human work. The power of destruction comes into play wherever man desires to be a Titan, wherever he proposes to be autonomously self-creative and to throw off the ultimate sanctions. The Bible provides for this a parable in the story of the tower of Babel. The tower that was erected in Babylon was actually a tremendous creative accomplishment of the ancient world and it had certain technological features. But this tower found its place in history and thus gained an abiding symbolical value, not because it was the prototype of creative, technological achievement but rather because this achievement also had within it a very special and secret purpose grounded in the nature of humanity itself. For these men determined to perform this gigantic technological feat because they had deposed God and with Promethean defiance were bent upon building a tower which would soar into the realms of the heavens from which they supposed they had banished him.

They wished to erect an architectural symbol of their own super-humanity. When man falls into megalomania and hubris, this frequently expresses itself in a kind of architectural gigantism. But then something extremely significant appeared: contrary to all the plans, the tower was incapable of constituting a center that would gather and bind men together. Quite to the contrary, the fate of dispersion and confusion of tongues swept down upon them. But was this really "fate," was not this confusion and dispersion the result of an offense, a sin?

The people who have deposed God and determined upon their own super-humanity can no longer trust each other. They know that now each one of them is subject only to the dictatorship of his own will to power and no longer bound to an ultimate authority. That makes him unpredictable and therefore one is bound to be afraid of him. The fear that destroys trust in Babylon and permits the terror of the unpredictable to triumph does not unite men; it rather drives them apart. Fear always has a centrifugal tendency. When man himself has become unpredictable and sinister, the technological enhancement of his power only makes him more sinister. If one cannot trust the normal man, then much less can one trust the man who has enhanced his greatness and power by means of technology. Once man has become an unpredictable and sinister being, then the moment he acquires a bow and arrow he is even more to be feared, and he reaches the pinnacle of sinisterness when he is equipped with atomic power.

Thus as the tower of Babel is a monument of man's greatness, it is at the same time a symbol of his sinisterness. The same is true of technology. In technology the qualities of its producer emerge with gigantic clarity. May not this explain the strange fact that, even though the technology of communication has diminished distances and brought people and nations closer to one another, this has by no means contributed to the growth of the solidarity of mankind? The warm, secure world, which really should result when nations have become neighbors through technological means, obviously has failed to appear.

The conclusion that must be reached here is this: Our technology is all right—simply because it is exact and based upon calculations—but obviously *man* is not all right, because he is incalculable, because he is unpredictable. And he is incalculable and unpredictable because he has thrown off the ultimate authority, or to put it quite plainly, because he has thrown off the commandments of God.

This brings us to the question whether technology is really a menace to man, or whether man, whose arm has been extended by technology, has not rather become a menace to himself, which would mean that the talk about the demonic character of technology is simply foolish, a kind of red herring thrown down to escape moral responsibility. In the last analysis it is not a matter of how atomic energy can be tamed, but rather of how man can be tamed, or more precisely, how he can be set straight. And for this there is no ready-made prescription; it is a question for every individual. Because man, who is at issue here, is always the same, so the great truths that stand above his life are always the same; they are always as young as the stars of the firmament which have been shining above him since time immemorial. The Book of Christianity will never grow obsolete although the old world is surpassed technologically and even the modern age is thrown into the discard.

Having thus stated at the outset that the problem of technology is exclusively a problem of *man*, we may now say that we have perhaps overshot the mark a bit. That is to say that this may put us in danger of jumping to a hasty conclusion. The conclusion runs something like this: If we see to it that man is set straight, then his technology will be all right too. And this, of course, is very often said in Christian sermons and exhortations. I, however, consider this attempt to attribute all the technological troubles of the atomic age *only* to human sin and to get at them *only* by appeals to the inner man to be an oversimplification. And to make clear the danger involved in this oversimplification I would merely remind you of what we said above concerning the "revolt of the means" and the autonomous elements in the technological process. It follows from these observations that man is by no means merely an autonomous subject who produces technological processes, but that he is at the same time drawn into a relationship of dependence upon them and becomes an object of these processes.

This is precisely what gives rise to that dramatic and exceedingly disturbing question of where in the midst of all these inexorable processes one's own decision of conscience has any chance at all. He who does not ask this question and is not determined to wrestle with it never even approaches the real mysteries of our age. At most he can be only a fellow traveler, not a shaper of this age. And even his activity would be basically no more than laissez-faire.

The crux of this whole question lies in the concept of what we have called *autonomy*. Is there really such a thing as the autonomy of technological development, of economics, of politics? And if it really exists, how can there be any real chance for responsible action, meaning free action inspired by conscience? Arnold Gehlen once said with a certain right that the scientist, as well as the technologist, appears to have been disfranchised in so far as he has no control over the work of research and application which he carries on. Strictly speaking, he is not the researcher who pushes forward his research; it is rather the research that pushes itself forward. And, what is more, it moves in accordance with a chain reaction which operates in an automatic process that proceeds from particular questions to particular answers and from there to a new set of questions. For the researcher neither "sets" the problems nor "decides" to apply technologically what he has learned. What becomes the problem follows by an inevitable necessity from what is already known, and it is of the logic of experiment that exact knowledge already includes control of the (technological) effect. The "decision" to apply the knowledge is unnecessary; or perhaps one might say that it is taken away from him. Oppenheimer, one of the builders of the atom bomb, once went beyond this and also described this logical inexorability as an irresistible psychical gradient when he said with regard to his own particular task that what is technologically "sweet" turns out to be irresistible even when it is the computation and construction of the atom bomb.

The *first* form in which the autonomy of technology operates is therefore the combination of question and answer, of theoretical knowledge and technological effect. One necessarily follows the other. The researcher appears to be only the medium through which this sequence operates. His own intellectual contribution emerges only from the ability (sometimes the ability of genius) to recognize the "waiting" chain reaction of question and answer and to resolve it. But is he really the responsible steersman? Does not the intellectual ship of scientific and technological progress sail on with nobody on the bridge?

The *second* form in which the autonomy of technology operates is expressed in the process which we may characterize by the
words "stress" and "counterstress." This process can be traced
in politics and economics as well as technology. We mention a
few examples:

When some important technological advance, let us say automation, is introduced into one sector of an industry, then the
companies in the same business must "follow suit" in order to
meet competition. Here we have an illustration of the relationship of stress and counterstress that operates with all the in-
evitability of natural law. Or we may think of the same law as
it operates in the realm of armaments. If a potential enemy
acquires atomic weapons, I am subjected to the necessity of
doing the same thing, or at least producing an equal force, for
my own self-defense. If I consider this armament to be madness
—and who does not?—then I cannot meet my responsibility for
combatting this madness by simply omitting to exert my "counterstress." This, after all, would only stimulate the potential enemy's
megalomania. Rather, I can put into practice my responsibility
of conscience over against this madness only by considering
political measures to bring about controlled disarmament. But
then this disarmament is itself subject to the law of stress and
counterstress; it is a process the individual phases of which are
likewise bound to the law of reciprocity.

If one stops and looks at the history of the world from this
point of view, one discovers that this law of stress and counterstress, this *do ut des*, "I give that you may give," this tit for tat,
permeates all spheres of life, even the personal relationship between my neighbor and myself. Only he who sees this clearly
can appreciate what a radically new thing it was that appeared
when the Gospel came. For the Gospel abolishes this law of
retaliation and reciprocation and makes way for the I-Thou relationship. It breaks this vicious circle and in the Golden Rule
lays upon me the obligation to make a fresh start and take the
free, venturesome initiative. But that which here can come like
a fresh, creative breeze into my relation to my neighbor and

make all things new is something that can be carried over only in a limited way into the more impersonal spheres of technology, economics, and politics. The endeavor to think through this distinction between these two spheres of life, not simply to separate them and let them fall apart, but rather to distinguish between them—this endeavor constitutes one of the most difficult and challenging chapters of theological ethics in both confessions.

❧ 23 ❧

Our Freedom and Our Free Time

In the last hundred years the main question that men have asked was this: "What can we do to contribute to social and technological progress?" If I am not mistaken, however, the real problem today is not primarily that of progress, but rather of going back and getting hold of the substance of what it means to be a human being in order to have something by which to evaluate our progress. Otherwise time simply evaporates, indeed, it becomes a boring, irksome thing. This is not at all hard to understand, for technological and social progress has given us a considerable reduction in the time we must devote to work; it has given us free time, leisure. But do we know what to do with it? Just consider the trouble we have dealing with our free time as this is reflected in certain of our figures of speech. We speak of "passing the time away" or of having to "kill time."

What is it really that we pass away, what is it that we kill? Obviously we do this only to something that is a mortal threat, something that is hostile to us. When we use these phrases we are really saying that we look upon time as a kind of enemy. And the fact is, of course, that when one no longer knows why one is living, when one has lost the meaning of life, then time does become an enemy. Then time reminds us that one day *finis* will come for us; it makes us aware of our finitude, and uncovers the dreadful inner emptiness that threatens us whenever we have nothing to do. Naturally, we can still take flight into "busyness," and the tempo of our life is already rather rapid. But where are we going, in what direction are we moving? Is not the movement that of a carrousel that always returns to the place where it started and moves us with great speed, but never takes us anywhere?

Hence we should reflect upon the question of leisure time not merely from the standpoint of how we should fill it up, of how we should occupy ourselves and plan our spare-time amusements; we should rather allow this problem to confront us with the deepest questions of our life, above all the question of the *meaning of life*.

As one who has always lived with young people and therefore does not speak only from an "old man's" point of view, I should like to bring out in more detail this ultimate background of the problem of leisure time.

Though all the world cries for a reduction in working hours —the executives as well as the workers—we are still faced with the paradoxical fact that we are afraid of the resulting free time. Sunday in particular is for many people a specter that makes them feel uneasy and depressed. As is well known, Jean-Paul Sartre has pointed out man's *dread of freedom*, and what he is saying is that man hardly knows what to do with his freedom. Perhaps down underneath he doesn't want it at all, but rather feels more secure in the apparatus that guides and takes care of him.

Drawing a parallel to what Sartre has said, one might also speak of man's *dread of free time*. In both cases the dread has the same root. We are all more or less in the habit of allowing our lives to be steered from outside of ourselves—by the radio, the television, all kinds of organizations and bureaus which arrange our vacations and our trips for us. We tend to be quite willing to play a role which is assigned to us by a stage director. We want nothing but to go on functioning—functioning smoothly, of course—in our work and our free time.

Pascal once said (and after all, that was about three hundred years ago): "All the unhappiness of men arises from one single fact, that they cannot stay alone quietly in their own chamber." Students say they cannot stand to be alone in their rooms; they need to screen out the dread with the noise of the radio. Even the pair of lovers on the edge of the woods have nothing more to talk about, so they bring along a portable radio to get the stimulation of jazz rhythms and make up for the lack of conversation. Even in love they can no longer travel under their own steam but have to be "sent" erotically. This implies two disastrous consequences.

First, it is possible for a person to allow himself to become completely outer-directed. A plant grows from within, from the center of its organism. It assimilates the energy of the sunlight and the earth and transforms it into its own substance. But it is possible for a man to become empty and stripped of all individuality, so that he constantly allows himself to be filled with foreign matter from the outside, such as the impressions made by picture magazines, advertising lights, noise, music, and rhythms. In fact, the result is a vicious circle, for he must constantly grow emptier in order to make room for these surging impressions.

Second, this destitution of the man who has become completely sterile and passive is immediately exploited by a particular kind of "manager" who uses it as a source of money. In other words, industrially produced articles for recreation are thrown upon the market—assembly-line music on the radio, "musical tutti-frutti," "gems of music," and whatever else the sounds that come rolling out at me may be called. I need not describe it any further. It suffices that one can get recreation and diversion services any time one wants them. The demand for musical consumers' goods and organized entertainment exceeds all bounds, and entertainers of all kinds, from operatic tenors to emcees, rush about from place to place in trains and planes to fill a vacuum here or banish some boredom there, and by doing so turn recreation more and more into amusement and diversion. The amusement business sees to it that hardly anybody can really enjoy himself any more. For real, liberating joy grows from the abundance of the heart, and not from some external titillation of the diaphragm that collapses like an empty inner tube as soon as one stops pumping it up from the outside and the entertainer-masseurs stop kneading and slapping it. *Therefore I should like to challenge young people especially to rebel against this racket.* This call to revolution can be expressed quite simply: Don't let others entertain you; do something yourselves, whether you dance or sing or play music or put on a play. It doesn't matter whether any of it is good enough to put on the stage. Far more important is doing something together and working on these things that bring you together and liberate you from the cursed role of always being nothing but passive objects and empty pots for the professional amusement functionaries. Such a project entered into together will develop your own talents and show you who you are; it will show you how rich and fascinatingly fine life can be.

This does not mean that we are crying up opposition to the radio and television. But every youth leader and everybody who has any responsibility for young people should regard it as his basic task to educate them to make the right choices among the many appeals that come to people today through the loudspeakers, television screens, and slot machines of all kinds. The coming elite will be an elite of ascetics, not in the sense of a negation of life but rather of a higher affirmation of life. Arnold Gehlen once said, "Today asceticism must call us to heroic goals [it therefore must not be negative!]. And today these goals consist in avoiding the obvious popular appeal, 'the low-voltage substitute-life.' "

Naturally it would be foolish to say to a youngster: "Don't keep the radio on all the time! Don't always run to the movies! Don't spend all your time staring at the TV!" Such appeals to forgo and abstain are of no avail whatsoever if a person does not acquire something that means more to him than all this, if he does not have good companions with whom he can put himself to the test in common projects. So I say once more: "Don't let others entertain you; do something yourselves!"

The second enemy we would like to combat is somewhat more difficult to describe because I do not want to step too hard on anybody's toes. I shall be politely cautious and call it "motor unrest." I choose this technical term intentionally in order not to cast any aspersions upon anybody's love for such vehicles as automobiles and motor bikes. Anyone who has loved to ride a motorcycle as much as I have—and even made his honeymoon trip on such a vehicle—would certainly be wary of disparaging it. And I can also understand that between the ages of fifteen and twenty one loves to go full speed, enjoys the multiplication of one's own power, scorns the miserable pedal-pusher on the sidewalk, and even loves to open up the muffler to make a big noise to make all the slowpoke pedestrians scatter before this motorized prince of the underworld. I'm not going to fulminate against all this; there are others who can do that. I would rather concentrate my attack upon this one point, namely, that this "motor unrest" causes us to run away from ourselves and to cultivate driving as an end in itself.

The positive side of my attack upon "motor unrest" can be put in this way: Cars and motor bikes are not for riding as such, but for getting somewhere, for arriving at a goal. Then when you get there you start walking. As a matter of fact, in this program we concur with the youth movement of former days. And the young person today is still just as eager to experience life and just as fearful that he may miss something. It ought not to be too difficult to provide him with a living example, and to show him that the maximum content of this experience is not realized in an amusement park or by rushing full speed past the beauty of trees and sky, but rather in activities in which all his faculties are challenged and developed—in overnight camping, hiking, enjoying the countryside, mountain climbing, the twilight hour in front of a tent, and in everything else that young people do on their trips, everything they learn about trees and people and animals. All this will be much less romantic than it was in the youth movement of the past, for we are no longer so naïve as we once were. But young hearts will always yearn for what Lynceus, the tower-warder, saw, according to Goethe's account. They must go out into the world in order to find themselves; they must roam in order to be sure of themselves. For the theorem that a straight line is the shortest distance between two points is really true only in mathematics.

> I gaze at the far,
> I look at the near,
> The moon and the stars
> The wood and the deer.
> I see in it all
> The beauty eternal,
> And as it delights me
> I delight in myself.
>
> *Faust* II, 5

But one does not see "the beauty eternal" in the mass consumption of landscape to which our "motor unrest" reduces us, any more than a person can "see" and appreciate a painting if he rushes through a gallery trying to take it all in at once with eyes that have become nothing more than snap-shooting machine guns. How poor are the people who let themselves be spewed out of a bus for a few moments in some renowned landscape at Königssee or in Upper Salzburg to be led about in groups through castles and rose gardens and then—naturally after mailing a few picture post cards—be sucked back as by a great vacuum sweeper into their waiting bus! And a hundred yards from these fat pastures of the tourist industry, where the landscape lies waiting and the crickets are chirping, not a soul is to be found. The poor flock of tourists, however, who have allowed themselves to be used as spectators by professional producers putting on a beauty contest of mountain peaks, castles, and lakes, come home worn out, with nothing to tell about, and, if the truth were known, having really experienced nothing at all. The person who swallows a noble wine as if it were lemonade gets no enjoyment and he is the one who is cheated. That's why we should walk and use the motor merely as a means to take us where we want to go. We must combat "motor unrest," not because motors are bad (they are certainly wonderful things!) but rather because when they get in the way they cheat us of real experience.

We might express what we are driving at here in a brief formula. The first act in the social drama was the struggle to obtain the opportunities to live like human beings. In order to gain these opportunities our fathers—and not least the labor unions—first had to create certain social conditions which would safeguard the economically weak from exploitation. The second act in the social drama, however, is now the utilization of these opportunities. And among them is the way in which we use the time gained by shorter working hours, namely, our leisure time. If we do not make good use of these opportunities, then the first act in this struggle has been in vain and we sink into the boredom of a perfected welfare state.

What, then, should we do? The worst thing of all would be for companies or unions or schools or the state to come in and organize something in the nature of public leisure-time entertainment and launch a new "Strength through Joy" movement. Nothing could be easier than this! There would be grateful customers, and we have always been masters at organizing. But this would only make things worse. For it would only make people more dependent upon outer-direction and more addicted to the drugs of self-forgetfulness. Or to express it in political terms, it would increasingly depersonalize people and turn them into a helpless, driven herd; it would transform them into mere human material to be kneaded and molded at will. Therefore one cannot organize leisure time. But one can organize something else: one can work in a planned way (and this, after all, is the meaning of organization) toward *enabling people to employ their leisure time meaningfully*.

The strategy to achieve this end would be this: we must first establish the areas in which leisure time is spent. And these areas are first, the family (with a high degree of priority), and second, particularly in the case of young people, the organizations which they join, their unions, for example, or clubs and societies, such as athletic clubs.

As regards the family, to my mind everything depends—and this is requirement number one—upon gathering together young parents and literally (I do not hesitate to use the word, though it is unpopular) giving them instruction in how to structure their family life. In my own family the children are read to for an hour almost every day. An adult must be available for this. It works, too, even though there is plenty going on in our house. Could not companies or unions or already existing clubs give instruction to young parents concerning *what* is to be read? Could not printed suggestions be made and books mentioned which are available in public libraries? Actually there are available good books for reading aloud which even indicate the number of minutes it takes to read each story. The finest radio program for children (and often they are very fine!) cannot compare with a story that is read or even told by someone in the home. Why should we not be able to train real grandmothers to read and tell stories instead of the mechanized "grandmothers" who tell recorded stories? What is needed is the realization of what is at stake and the will to do it. Then it will work.

When one has read something, one can also talk about it. Then, besides the direct impression, which the far more perfect radio presentation can never replace, there will come into being a human atmosphere of trust and togetherness.

Likewise, parents ought to be encouraged to play with their children, to go on expeditions, to search for mushrooms, or to collect stamps. I believe that we would be surprised at how parents would respond to such instructional meetings and how much they themselves would again become children with flushed and happy faces. All that is needed is to make a start and provide some examples. Down underneath everyone is grateful when he has been given guidance to do something meaningful, and can go to bed at night with the feeling that the day has been orderly and substantial. The person who day after day consumes nothing but the diet of the picture magazines and newspapers ends up with nothing but anemia of the brain and a moral hangover.

As for the second area, that of organizations, the task is perhaps easiest among the athletic associations. If they have a good coach or trainer, they provide meaningful activity. But it is possible to use them merely to provide a show for the spectators. The fact that one may become a local star and thus a cut-rate edition of a celluloid star is the least of its pleasures, though it can be nice. Far more important is the satisfaction of being able to do something with one's own strength, the recreation that comes from it, and the happiness of comradeship with one's fellow players. And what a pleasure it is to discuss things with one another and in the process acquire one's own opinions and learn to express them. Are there really no persons who are willing to set themes for groups of young people—all the way from political questions to the problems of young rebels, from modern art to Adenauer and Brandt? There are so many admirable schools of public speaking that give courses which help people to overcome shyness, teach them to speak and discuss, and provide other opportunities for building successful personality. Isn't it possible, instead of being merely passive recipients, to take all this ourselves and spread it among active, vital groups?

I could go on and mention many more such suggestions, but far more important than the suggestions is the basic thought that must inform them (which is the reason why I intended all that I have said merely to serve as examples), namely, that we build communities in which we teach people *to do something themselves* and immunize them against dependence upon the professional amusement functionaries. Do not object that these will always be very small groups. Anybody who is afraid of small numbers will never accomplish anything. In fact, one should not even plan to do this on a large scale. The sociological law that must operate here is rather that in which a group of people start somewhere and form a model. This then becomes contagious and propagates itself either by cell-division or by bulb-formation. Everything that has become great and challenging in the world began in this way.

This brings me, so to speak, to the end, but I cannot close without quoting and giving a positive application to a statement once made by Carlo Schmid: "Only he who knows what to do with himself can do something with his leisure time." But who is it that knows what to do with himself? A person who performs his daily stint of work and amusement in routine fashion and then suddenly conks out because he has fallen asleep? Certainly not he! I can know what to do with myself and obtain some verve and clarity of purpose in my life only if I know why I am here, only if I know the meaning of my life.

But what is the meaning of our lives? Isn't it strange that this question is so seldom asked? When we go to the movies we ask: "What's playing?" But how many of us ask: "What's playing in my life? How is the producer? Who or what is playing the chief role? Is mere chance perhaps the producer, the director of what happens in my life?"

But if this is so, how do I come to respect human beings as having value in themselves and recognize any such thing as humanity at all? Each one of us can answer that question only with the ultimates he has experienced in his own life. All our human values of function and fitness perish and pass away:

> Are you proud of blooming cheeks,
> Aglow with milk and crimson?
> Ah, the roses die and fade away.

The attraction of youthful beauty does not last forever, and we feel the touch of sadness when we think of the dull, drab decades that young beauty queens may have ahead of them. Sickness, suffering, and guilt have never yet spared anyone, and the time comes when the value of our lives diminishes in the eyes of many.

Then everything depends upon whether there is something in our lives that remains true to us, that never lets us down, something that inspires and gives substance to our youth, and consoles and stays us as we grow older, something that is *always* there.

Albert Einstein once said that we live in an age of perfect means and confused ends. Therefore everything depends upon our setting up, not merely work-goals, but also an ultimate goal of life, and keeping this goal always in view. The man who merely goes on living and never asks what is the meaning of this life is like a man who tells pointless stories. "What's playing?" That's the question I had to ask again before we close. I have indicated what my own answer to it is. We must never allow the question to cease stirring within us.

❧ 24 ☙

The Origin of Man: Questions on the Border Between Religion and Science

It would be fine if I could believe that God created the world, that he takes an interest in me and is thinking his higher thoughts about me. But can I believe the ancient words of the Bible concerning the creation of man without doing violence to my intellectual conscience? For, after all, the Bible says that man was formed of dust from the ground. And I know it to be a fact that man came into being altogether differently; I know that life on earth is millions of years old, and that man also developed upward from animality in an unimaginably long process. Does not faith with its mythical, legendary conceptions occupy the short end of the seesaw over against science, which has long since put biological development in the place of these ancient, outmoded conceptions of creation—and done so by means of exact evidence?

This is the question as commonly stated. It seems to me, however, that scientific doubt of belief in creation is based upon a completely wrong way of putting the question. That is to say,

I can *either* ask where man came from biologically and receive the answer that he sprung from prehuman animal forms, *or* I can also ask *to what purpose* he is here, what he was intended to be, what is the point of his existence. If I ask the latter question, the answer I get from the Bible is that man was designed to be a child of God, that he was intended for fellowship with God. Then it becomes apparent that these two questions must not be mixed together. They lie on different levels. And therefore they also do not express an *either-or*—any more than it is a mutually exclusive *either-or* for me to say on the one hand: "The *St. Matthew Passion* is a musical form of worship," and on the other: "The *St. Matthew Passion* is a sequence of physically measurable sound vibrations." These two statements also lie on different levels and in their way both are true.

Once this is clearly understood, we arrive at the following consequences. I do not offend against faith when I say that man developed from the animal over a period of millions of years. How could *one* truth (that of science) contradict *another* truth (that of faith)? No, I offend against faith only when I dare to assert that I can derive the *nature* of man, his destiny, the meaning of his life from his animal origin. For when I attempt to do this, the answer I arrive at is that man is only a higher mammal; he is perhaps a beast of prey; but in any case he is determined by the instincts of food-seeking, acquisition, and sex. Then world history becomes a separate chapter in general zoology. So we see what are the consequences of that position.

But this must be stated even more precisely. Naturally, I am not denying that—from the biological point of view—man is a mammal. But *only* from the biological point of view. Surely according to his nature he is something more and something different—unless we are willing to say that a mother's love for her child is no more than ape-love and that man's death is the same as the death of an animal. Is not sexuality, too, something completely different from what it is in our fellow animal creatures? Naturally, human sexuality has its biological side, but it is certainly more than this. For something completely different has been introduced into the biological receptacle of instinctual processes of procreation; what takes place here is, after all, my relation to the person who is closer to me than anybody else in the world. In a sexual way I love and serve him. In a sexual way I become indebted to him. In a sexual way I fail him and suffer shipwreck. In a sexual way I experience fulfillment and defeat in my relation to him. In short, in my loving and hating, in my delinquencies and faults I am acting altogether as a *human being*, not as an animal. The biological is, as it were, only a receptacle that contains a completely and exclusively human I-thou relationship and is therefore full of love and devotion but also of guilt and rejection, just as it is (except that it has a different biological emphasis) everywhere else in my life, wherever I deal with my fellow man, no matter whether he be my boss or my employe, my neighbor or my colleague.

Whenever I make this "receptacle" of the *bios* the "content" and thus turn it into an end in itself, whenever I say that this instinctual, physical side is the end, the thing itself, then sexuality becomes inhuman, then it becomes excessively a blind urge and sexual intercourse becomes nothing more than the attempt to quench my sexual thirst. And my partner then becomes nothing more than a glass of water which I gulp down and then perhaps cast away. Then my partner is no longer a human being and certainly not a neighbor, but merely a thing, a mere instrument.

So these are the consequences I arrive at when I employ science, not merely as a source of information concerning how man came into being biologically, but go beyond this and turn it into a substitute for faith, expecting it to tell me what is my destiny and the meaning of my life. This it cannot tell me. Bolshevism demonstrates what results when science nevertheless attempts to do so, and what happens to the kind of science that attempts to do so.

This is why the Bible, even where it speaks of the creation of man, speaks in picture language less of his origin than of his goal, the purpose of his creation. This is made clear to us with monumental simplicity in Psalm 139:

There is One who has blessed us and bestowed this gift upon us through the mediation of nature, in the same way that he broadcasts the signs of his grace through the dew and the sunshine, through the rainbow and the winds.

And then, once one has grasped this, it would seem to me not too difficult also to see that faith and science do not contradict each other at all, simply because their affirmations lie on different levels. Can we not say of mankind as a whole what we have just said of the birth of this *one* child, this *one*, specimen of "mankind"? Can we not say this in almost the same words that were used in Psalm 139? Thou didst know man when he was still no more than unformed substance, mere protoplasm, or perhaps a *euhomininen*, an antecedent form of *homo sapiens*. Then at a definite point in this development lasting millions of years, thou didst call him by his name, and make thyself known to him; thou didst summon him before the majesty of thy face to bestow upon him that unique dignity of humanity which thou didst not give to any animal.

This one point at which God caused man to emerge from the ranks of all other creatures and made him something unique is described in what is really our text: "God . . . breathed into his nostrils the breath of life; and man became a living being." Here this earthy creature, still bound within universal creatureliness, which the Bible presents in the symbol of "dust from the ground," here this prehuman, still unformed substance was breathed upon by the breath of another world and translated into that realm which we call human life. I have always felt that Michelangelo's portrayal of man's becoming man in his famous painting in the Sistine Chapel is a singularly profound exposition of the creation of man. Adam, the man, is already there; but he is, so to speak, not yet there as a man in the *real* sense. He is still a candidate for manhood. He lies half erect, still in a dreamy stupor, though his face is turned to the Father-God in questioning expectation. His leg is already tautened to rise, and all is prepared for him to rise up in the next instant and face God. But between these two instants a miracle must occur—the miracle

For thou didst form my inward parts,
   thou didst knit me together in my mother's womb.
I praise thee, for thou art fearful and wonderful.
   Wonderful are thy works!
Thou knowest me right well;
   my frame was not hidden from thee,
When I was being made in secret . . .
Thy eyes beheld my unformed substance;
   in thy book were written, every one of them,
the days that were formed for me,
   when as yet there was none of them.

Here one thing is crystal clear: the Psalmist is speaking
the biological origin of man. We might therefore say that he
referring to the mammalian side of man, suggesting the myste
of the meeting of sperm and ovum. But, after all, this is only
biological sphere within which something totally different tal
place; that is to say, within which God utters his creative wo
"Let there be!" and behold, it is there, it comes into being–
come into being. I lived in his heart, a completed image, wh
I was still a microscopically small, unformed embryonic spec
even then he had already called me by my name, already he h
designed for me my days to come, my life history, my talen
and my role, already he had called me to himself. *This*, after a
is the point of the passage.

And is not this basically simple to understand? What are your
parents doing when they send out a birth announcement sayin
"God has blessed us with our first child"? Surely they do n
mean that God sent a baby directly from heaven. They are we
aware of the processes of conception and birth, the ecstasies
love and the biological operations that brought forth this chil
What they are trying to say in this announcement, however,
something totally different: God in his goodness has given u
this child by way of the "biological." For, after all, it was h
who gave us the *bios* itself. "It passes through our hands, but
comes from God," said Matthias Claudius. God's gifts come t
us through our bodies, through and by way of physiological law

of the spark of the Spirit leaping from the outstretched finger of the Creator to man. Without this miracle he would have remained an earthbound creature and would never have become the wanderer between two worlds which he was designed to be. He may perhaps have been a higher kind of creature (how beautiful is Michelangelo's "man" even before he became man!) but he would still have been something other than the man who is privileged to be God's child and partner. Michelangelo portrays, as it were, the last moment of pre-man, the *euhomininen*. And not until the next instant does he become a man, a child, a brother, a neighbor—the image of God and at the same time one of whom "it does not yet appear what he shall be" (cf. I John 3:2). For God is not yet done dealing with man and his history goes on—to the world's last day and beyond it to eternity.

❧ 25 ❧

What Does It Mean to Take God Seriously?

There are many different kinds of temperament and character among people. There are thousands of shades and variations of faith and doubt in which we face God and his world. Here we wish to speak of one kind, a very common one, and the man who represents it.

He is the typical spectator, the man who sees everything from the outside. He observes and analyzes the course of the world and declares that God is hard and unjust; he says that God is merely the personification of unpredictable fate. He wants to reap what he did not sow. He wants to reap faith, for example. But what does he ever give to me that would make anything like faith grow within me? When I look at life, this man says, it is very hard for me to believe that there is One above us who is thinking higher thoughts about us, that there is a God of love. When four small children are robbed of their mother through the act of a drunken driver—what kind of meaningful providence is that, where is there the slightest note of love in a thing like that? And what about the larger history of the world? Is it not brutal self-interest that prevails there, perhaps even the cold autonomism of process, such as that of technological development? Or take the church; is the state of the church with its dubious human failings and its impotent talk a thing to strengthen anybody's faith? How can God expect to reap faith when he sows such miserable little reason for faith?

"Yeah, where are you going to get anything without stealing?" says St. Joan of the Slaughter House in Bert Brecht's play. "Gentlemen," she says, "there is also such a thing as moral purchasing power. Raise the purchasing power of morality and you'll get the morality too."

This is the way this spectator-Christian thinks too. He waves you off and says resignedly: "God ought to raise the purchasing power of religion; he ought to give us some plain proofs of the Spirit and of power, then he'd get some religion, then he'd have our faith!"

But if there is one thing that is certain, it is this: It is impossible to "know" God by observing life and analyzing history and the like and then saying that, if we should find him in this way, then we will take him seriously, then we will be active in his cause and make him the standard of our life. It is just the opposite: only he who takes him seriously ever knows him at all. No one else ever knows him.

But how can one take him seriously when one knows nothing about him? Well, I should say that one should deal with God in exactly the same way that the nobleman dealt with his servants in the parable of the pounds (Luke 19:27). The nobleman said, "I will condemn you out of your own mouth." In other words: I will meet you and discuss this with you on your own level. In exactly the same way we should say to God: "I will convict you by what you yourself have said. Let it be your own words that either convince me or with which I rout you and show up your absurdity. Here are your words: "Cast all your cares on me, for I care for you." Very well, I'll do this and test it out. I have some cares. I'm afraid of tomorrow and next week. This time I won't read my daily and weekly horoscope; instead I'll pour out my fears to you. I'll try you out, God, this once. You ought to be worth an experiment. I'll see whether you really can get me through tomorrow and next week. I'll find out whether you really will build paths for me when the going is hard, whether you really will put rod and staff in my hand in the dark valleys, whether you really will see to it that I do not lose trust in your guiding hand in the darkest moments when I cannot see either the bridge or the path, the shepherd or the staff."

To take God seriously means to take him at his word and to give him the opportunity to respond in the way he has promised to do in his Word. We can never receive anything with clenched fists or drooping arms. We must be willing to stretch out our hands and "open our mantle wide," as Luther once said.

Perhaps we may have to start by praying like this: "Lord God (if you do exist), at your word (if you really said it), I pray to you (if you can really hear me) to forgive my sin, to be with me in my fear, to comfort me in my loneliness, to show me my neighbor, to warm my heart with love, and in all the good and the hard places, the heights and the depths in my life let me feel your hand—the hand that reaches out for me and leads me, the hand that lifts my burdens, that smooths the troubled brow and makes death easy because my head can rest in it. Tomorrow I will arise and trade with my pounds for you and serve my neighbor as if you really existed. Then you will break through the great silence that surrounds you and suddenly you will be with me."

That's the way it is with God: when we listen God speaks, when we obey God acts. "Him who comes to me I will not cast out," says Jesus Christ. And for this word he died. So seriously did he take us. He deserves that we give him a chance.

❧ 26 ❧

The Animals

When I heard that there was a dog in Sputnik II, I had a silent conversation with my dachshund. I turned to him first because he happens to be the dog named "Axel" with whom my children play and who after every trip welcomes me back with boundless, unreserved joy—a joy that is a bit of remembrance of paradise. And I thought: It's a good thing they didn't shoot you up and that you are still with us.

But then he suddenly became for me a representative of his whole species. He belongs, after all, to those beings which have allied themselves with man and become his friend. Sometimes it distresses me a bit that we Christians have so little to say about our obligation toward the animals, for, after all, he makes his sun shine and sends his rain for them too. He is not only the Lord of the good and the evil, but also the Lord of those who live beyond good and evil. And if love is something that gives of itself and has compassion upon the weaker, then undoubtedly it also means love for helpless creatures.

For surely the greatness of man, to which he has been called and which gives him dominion over the earth, should not manifest itself in brutal oppression of the animals, but rather in his superiority over them. This superiority consists in the fact that man is conscious of himself, that he can lay hold of and also miss his destiny, and that he can relate himself to him who gave him life. This the animals do not know and cannot do. But since man does know and can do this, since he can look up to his Creator, the world of creatures has become a responsibility entrusted to his care.

"The man gave names to all cattle, and to the birds of the air, and to every beast of the field," we read in the account of creation. This probably means that man also called the animals by these names. There is something like a fellowship with them. In the world which was still intact and whole, all created things stand together under God. Man stands under God knowingly, the animals unknowingly. This superiority over the other creatures which is given and entrusted to man dare not be used against the creatures which have been subordinated to him. For if man exercises his dominion in the name of God, he can exercise it only in the name of that love which he himself receives and in the name of that care which God has for *all* his creatures.

But the world is not intact and whole. And if this is so, if the world of men lies in shadow, if Cain's fratricide and the tower of Babel fell like hoarfrost upon the morning of creation—what has this to do with the creatures, since they, after all, are beyond good and evil? Are not the animals exempt from this fate?

Paul once said something rather enigmatic concerning the "groaning" of all creation and suggested that it, too, was yearning and crying for redemption. What this means we cannot discuss here; it touches the ultimate mysteries. I should like only to mention how this saying of Paul's came home to me personally.

When I was a young man—before I ever bothered my head about the theological background of this saying—I once asked a venerable servant of God how he would explain this obscure passage. All he said was: "Look into the eyes of a dog and you will know."

Now I admit that this is not enough to explain such a passage, but since that time I have not ceased to meditate upon it. Whenever I look into the eyes of a dog and he into mine the thought comes back to me. And though we must guard against sentimentality and the tendency to read into it what is not there, I cannot shake off the conviction that real communication with creation takes place here. And the conversation runs something like this:

"You, my little dog, are a very special part of creation. For the fact is that both of us—unlike innumerable others of your fellow creatures—have come together in some remarkable way and now we are living together. If anything should happen to hurt you, I would be sad. And I am sure that if anything should happen to me, it would also grieve your dog's heart. You know exactly when something is depressing me. And when I am feeling cheerful you make the funniest efforts to show that you are happy with me. Sometimes from your eyes the mystery of the creatures looks out at me—so strongly, so movingly that it goes right through me. I keep thinking that it hurts you not to be able to express yourself and to tell me what you know. True, you can be very eloquent with all the movements of your body, your wagging tail, and your busy little feet. But you cannot speak. Sometimes you give me to understand that I do not understand you. There is a very deep river between us and we cannot get across to each other. And just because you are such a special bit of creation, just because your dog's lot is so bound up with my human lot, this wall of separation is all the more painful. We mean more to each other than I can say or you can bark. You are a speechless creature, and perhaps you are thinking: My master is a noseless creature."

Sometimes a dog can preach a sermon too. And the sermon he preaches is not inferior to that which little children, according to Jesus, can preach. I had a vivid experience of this on a ship coming to America. I mentioned this incident in another sermon, but I may repeat it here.

On the voyage over, a big shepherd dog was with us. His master had sent him over by ship since he himself was going by plane.

He was an exceedingly miserable dog. He was living in an unfamiliar world, a world of strange smells and strange people who meant nothing to him. The ground under his feet was unsteady, there were no trees, and the world ended at the railing. For him it was doubtless a plunge into Nothingness; his whole dog-world-view collapsed and he was pitched into the void. Looking at this dog, one no longer felt that the groaning of creation was merely a myth.

On the return voyage we again had a dog on board; this time a lap dog and really nothing more than a "half portion." But even though outwardly everything was just as bad for him, he did not generate the waves of sadness that the other dog did; for his master was with him. The little creature often fixed his eyes upon him and it was as if he were saying, "This is a crazy world and I have stopped trying to understand it. But as long as you are here it can't be too bad. The time will come when this will be over and then I'll smell some half way normal smells and see some trees too."

Precisely because there is such a thing as friendship between man and animal, this little animal preached a very powerful sermon on trust.

Also germane to this superiority of man over the animals is the fact that he feels shame when animals are made to suffer for him—whether the animal be an old cart horse, a watchdog, or the little creature in Sputnik II. I am not speaking here of the sorrowful struggle and fear in nature itself. That is a different matter. I am speaking only of the suffering that man inflicts upon his animals.

Why are we ashamed when we kill animals, experiment upon them, and cause them to suffer for us? Doubtless because animals cannot suffer ethically. We human beings are capable of giving meaning to our suffering. And even when we cannot understand it —as a martyr is privileged to understand his suffering—pain can nevertheless become a school in which we learn to trust God's "higher thoughts." The animal, however, suffers without the consolation of understanding and trust.

True, we dare not sentimentalize this matter. Certainly animal pain is quite different from ours. For precisely because the animal does not understand, it also has no sense of a future, but lives in the present moment. Thus the animal is spared the full impact of pain that we humans suffer when we anticipate future pain and endure the fear of our own finitude. And yet, even though the animal's pain is concentrated only upon the immediate moment—the cow immediately goes on feeding the moment after it has been frightened by a thunderclap—this moment is nevertheless filled with all the gravity of ununderstood pain or the termination of creaturely joy and well being. And this we human beings have done.

The shame that comes upon us when this happens is perhaps the last remnant of a devout dread that shrinks from injuring God's creation. It is doubtless also the last symptom of a knowledge that the world is no longer whole and intact, but that a great rift runs through not only the world of men, where infliction of pain, hostility, oppression, and intimidation are rife, but also the world of creatures.

Only the person who has some conception of the fact that we have the Fall behind us and that it is always a part of our heritage can have any comprehension of why this is so and why it is that in this world that keeps thrusting toward chaos we cannot get along without using force to punish, restrain, and to inflict pain. The very existence of the state and therewith the mandate of ordered self-preservation is such an emergency institution in a fallen world. The good can survive in this dubious world only if it is armored. And if the avenging forces were removed the evil mob would raise its insolent head and bring chaos crashing down upon us. The fact is that we live in a world of conflict. Only a visionary fanatic can fail to see that. And it is the goodness of God that he espouses these emergency institutions, that he spreads his rainbow of reconciliation over this questionable world, that nevertheless he permits it to go on living until it comes to the "dear last day."

It would therefore be wrong to use Albert Schweitzer's excellent statements concerning the sanctity of life in a sentimental and unrealistic way. Just as men cannot live together without sacrifice, so we cannot live with the creatures without sacrifice. It probably cannot be helped that animals must die in order to maintain human life. But we ought never to lose the sense of dread at the thought of the rift which runs through creation and that one must suffer if the other is to gain.

The carcasses of horses that strew the battlefields of men remain an indictment which declares that innocent creatures are drawn into the strife of men. And much is gained if our shame and sorrow over this never wholly disappears, even though there is no way to spare the creatures their misery in this world between the Fall and the Last Judgment. There should remain within us at least a grain of the knowledge that man as the lord of the earth does not have the right to deal with creation in this way, but rather that it is his original sin that makes him do so and that he is the source of the disorder that overshadows the cosmos.

There is also a perverse love for animals by which we dishonor the creatures. It is possible to become a sectarian enthusiast for the prevention of cruelty to animals and make of it a pseudo religion. This is always the case when we use the animals as a diversionary maneuver, in other words, when we become selfish animal-lovers and allow our fellow men to go in want, when we put cheap sentiment in the place of willingness to sacrifice.

There is a kind of love for animals which is a sign of profound degeneration. This degeneration consists in that we are no longer capable of real love, that we may even despise human beings and make the animal an idol.

The animals remind us of that whole and healthy world in which Adam gave names to his brother and sister creatures and spoke with them, that world which Francis of Assisi evoked when he preached to the birds as his beloved fellow creatures.

❧ 27 ❧
Theme Number 1 in Our Preaching

In our preaching we must bear in mind the changed intellectual situation in which we live. In times past people thought that knowledge was power. He who knows the laws of nature and understands how to apply them can rule the world; he is mightier than the others who are ignorant. With a few muskets and cannon it was possible to hold in check whole colonial peoples. For the white man "knew" more than the colored. Therefore he had power over them. In the meantime, however, it has become clear to us that the dictum "knowledge is power" is not correct. For our knowledge can become stronger than we ourselves are. And when that happens we are helpless before it. We see this in atomic science. We know more about the atoms than we can harness. Knowledge of the laws of nature allows man to call down the energies of the sun upon the earth and to build atom bombs. We have become so powerful that we are capable of turning our planet into a scattered cloud of dust in the universe.

Stated in this way, it is, of course, somewhat imprecise. We have said that knowledge of the laws of nature "allows" man to build such bombs. Strictly speaking, however, this is not quite true, for man's knowledge not only "allows" him to do this, but also "compels" him to do so. All nations dread the atom bomb. They are, so to speak, running away from their knowledge; for it has something sinister and menacing. So we can no longer say that man has gained power through his knowledge. One must rather say that his knowledge has become mightier than he himself is. And now he is even afraid that he will die of this knowledge.

Why, then, do men go on building atom bombs when they do not want them at all? They do so because they are afraid of each other. They are not afraid of the atom bomb itself, but of each other. And this fear becomes greater and greater the more they realize that others may become more powerful then they are. The other fellow may wipe out my whole country by pushing a single button. Therefore I too must have this terrible weapon. And so they keep bidding each other up. This we call the arms race. Nobody knows where it will end. Nobody wants it, but everybody thinks it is necessary.

I have mentioned this only because we can learn something very important from it, and that is that the dictum "knowledge is power" is obsolete. Knowledge itself is no problem for us. It progresses steadily and we know how to secure it: one must search and learn. Nor is power a problem for us. We know the way to gain it and how to bend nature by technical means, how to organize society, and how to safeguard ourselves against a dangerous monopolization of power by division of power. All this is no longer a fundamental problem. But in its place a different and totally new problem has arisen, and this is the problem of the "knower," the knowing man himself—precisely because he is afraid of his knowledge. He is also afraid of his peers. He has the anxious feeling that all his knowledge and skill is taking him on a flight where there is no known direction or destination and no stopping.

In times past men dreamed dreams of the future development of mankind; they foresaw a kingdom of peace and justice in which man would no longer have to work and technology would relieve him of all his burdens. Today, however, the poets and thinkers are devising nightmares; pictures of the end of the world caused by nuclear technology, of dictatorships in which the rulers control the entire lives of their subjects through television techniques, a world of artificially generated men and robots. Knowledge and skill are no longer a problem, but rather the knowing human being himself is the enigma. He is afraid of his own potentialities.

Why? Certainly because he is no longer bound to God and therefore must inevitably be drawn into hopeless and unpredictable adventure. Certainly because he no longer knows him to whom he can entrust himself, him who is concerned with his welfare, who loves him and is thinking his higher thoughts about him.

Knowledge, technological knowledge at any rate, is no longer a problem. But when the knowing human being loses his faith he becomes a problem to himself. Knowledge and faith belong together, for knowledge without faith creates fear.

Albert Einstein once said that we live in an age of perfect means and confused goals. We might go further and say that the means are no longer a problem since they are clearly directed toward perfection: we shall soon have social perfection and along with it perfect means of subsistence. We have perfect apparatus and techniques, but man is beginning to freeze to death because he has lost his goal. I am thinking of the story of the rich young ruler, who strove to secure perfect moral means and kept all the commandments from his youth but lost sight of the goal, and then threw himself at the feet of Jesus to find out what it was.

Everything depends—and this is our responsibility as the church—upon our arousing our fellow men to ask this question concerning the goal and then never growing weary of pointing them to the peace of the Father's house to which God is seeking to bring us home.

But here I must say something that weighs heavily on my heart. I think that I see a task which the church of Jesus Christ is disastrously failing to perform. It seems to me that instead the church is busying itself with all kinds of trivialities.

No one doubts that the church has learned much from the catastrophe in our recent history, including its ways of proclaiming the Gospel. It has established evangelical academies and made the Gospel to be heard as it applies to the problems of everyday life and vocation. It endeavors to make the commandments and consolations of God audible also in the realm of our earthly life. The church has taken a stand on the questions of armament and social organization because it knows that Jesus Christ is not only for the individual but that he died for the world. It has organized *Kirchentagen* (church congresses) on a large scale and employs all the means of technology from loudspeakers to motion pictures to proclaim its message. It is not my intention to criticize this fundamentally, however much there may be to find fault with in details. What I am concerned about is that the church of Jesus Christ, in its preoccupation with all that it has undertaken to do in this respect, may have forgotten something else that should mean far more to us than all the rest of this put together. If I am not greatly deceived, in the meantime God has already brought us to another station on the road.

What this is I should like to explain by relating an experience of my own that made me realize this one thing and laid it upon my conscience. I do my work of preaching in St. Michael's Church in Hamburg, that beautiful, spacious church whose green spire greets from afar the ships that come into Hamburg. Naturally, I am grateful and glad that many seeking people come here, that some of them may be comforted by what they hear, and take with them a bit of joy, and perhaps also learn to believe in him who has overcome the world and therefore also liberates men from anxiety and inquietude. And yet in the midst of this joy I have learned to know the poverty of the church: it does not have enough co-workers. Mission evangelism in the old style may still have a few outstanding advocates, but on the whole its time is beginning to run out. It concentrated essentially and very creditably upon awakening the congregation which had become somewhat torpid and sleepy, stirring up the indifferent, starting the contented, and comforting the doubting and despairing. That it was able to perform this task in the way it did was undoubtedly owing to the fact that the people who came to hear brought with them a store of knowledge which they had gained from confirmation and religious instruction. This needed only to be stirred into life; it needed, as it were, to be brought out of a state of incubation and given increased virility. Today the situation is different.

Today the person who has never heard of Goethe, Schiller, and Thomas Mann is considered uneducated. But who knows anything about Moses or Isaiah or Paul or even Christ? There are gaps in the knowledge of even so-called cultured people that are simply shocking. In one of my services there were two students who had never heard the Lord's Prayer. When the congregation prayed it together it made a tremendous impression upon them and they searched about to find the wording of it. Since the people around them seemed to know the prayer by heart they were ashamed to inquire about it. They went to the public library and then to the library of our theological faculty, but nowhere could they find the Lord's Prayer, only books about it. They concluded that it must be a tremendously familiar prayer, since everybody assumed that its wording was known to everybody else. They did not know that it might be found in the Gospels. Finally, the idea occurred to them that it might perhaps be spoken in the radio services, to which they had never listened before. So they sat down with a notebook before the loud-speaker to take it down. One day they told me about this, since I had them in frequently to talk about questions of faith. With beaming faces they said, "Now we have our Lord's Prayer!"

This may be rather exceptional, but it is not too unusual in many of the dechristianized areas of our country.

And here we are speaking the Word of God to these people. They sense perhaps that this is something they ought to have, that here they would find peace. But they do not know even the simplest passages of the Bible or the catechism. They hear the bells and want to come, but they do not know where they are. We must organize confirmation instruction for adults. This is "theme number 1" for the church.

Today books of facts and general knowledge are among the best sellers in the shops. People have a tremendous thirst for the basic elements of knowledge and factual information. What does the church have to offer at this point? We often moan about the fact that almost everywhere the church services do not draw the public and that those who do come are always the same people. But why should the others come when they have not the slightest understanding of the implications of what is being said in these services? All our efforts to modernize the language of our preaching are of no help whatsoever. We must furnish fundamentals, we must provide the plain bread of the catechism— fundamentals and more fundamentals!

In many of the larger cities the Roman Catholic church has a strategic reserve of theologians—not infrequently they are Jesuits—who are assigned exclusively to this service. We have now instituted such a course in Hamburg, and a whole group of university instructors have put themselves at the disposal of the program. The courses are so arranged that a series of topics which has been carefully considered and discussed beforehand is dealt with. The presentation of the topic is kept brief and most of the evening is devoted to discussion. At first we invited (by means of cards which I had distributed in St. Michael's Church) only persons between the ages of eighteen and thirty-five. Now we also have courses for those who are older, and mixed courses because the demand was so exceedingly great. In each case we planned the courses to extend over ten evenings. We also considered the place of meeting important: ample rooms with an atmosphere of privacy which would lend itself to something like a conversational mood. The participants were to be made to feel that they were not being called to depart from their normal style of living but rather being met on their own ground and in their own familiar atmosphere. We avoid every appearance which would suggest that these people are merely objects to be preached at or that they are being treated as an anonymous audience. The nature of these gatherings has also led to closer associations among those who took the courses. Sometimes they refused to stop when the ten evenings were up, and when their instructor actually had not the time to continue for several weeks, they went on by themselves without a leader. We are very happy with this outcome and we are constantly having to arrange for continuation courses.

In this connection I have observed that this question of style and atmosphere is exceedingly important where the susceptibility and receptiveness of modern people is concerned. Young people simply cannot be gotten into a dismal hall which is decorated without taste or even with cheap, sentimental pictures and Scripture passages burnt on wood. I do not consider it theologically "legitimate" (to use a vogue word) that these questions of style in our proclamation of the Gospel should be considered merely as having nothing to do with proclamation. The Word of God is certainly far more than merely the particular words which are acoustically audible in a room. The Word of God puts its stamp on the forms of community and molds our style of living, because it is intended to embrace our whole life. It is therefore no wonder that people who live on the fringes or beyond the horizon of the church are at first either attracted or repelled by these forms which have been stamped by the Word of God, in other words, by the peripheral, external side which the church presents. The minister who is not so proud that he desires only to preach, and who possesses enough humility also to be willing to ring the bells and at least get the attention of people so that they will listen, will not simply ignore or brush aside this external question of the form of proclamation.

All the many brethren who are occupying themselves with liturgical reforms, for whom it is a problem whether the minister should chant or speak and then in which key he should chant or speak, must certainly have our respect. But there are priorities and degrees of urgency in the kingdom of God too. Before we imitate the hosannas of the angel—with all due deference to the reform of worship—we ought to have compassion on the flocks that are without a shepherd.

But can we be preoccupied with cathedrals while outside souls are going under? A drop of compassion for the flocks who are without a shepherd is better than an ocean of theological knowledge and liturgical enthusiasm.

I am not advocating antiliturgical sectarianism and the destruction of images. But I wish in all earnestness to say this word about priorities. We dare not desire dessert while disdaining plain bread. "Otherwise they will die before we get to them," said the elder Bodelschwingh. And during the Third Reich Dietrich Bonhoeffer once said, "Only he who speaks out for the Jews dare also chant in Gregorian." And when he said that, he was addressing himself in his situation to this same problem of priorities in what is urgent and permissible.

❧ 28 ❧

The Joy of Repentance

When we address ourselves to the theme of the Day of Repentance we find ourselves in a rather helpless situation. The word "repentance" is a poor translation of the Greek word *metanoia*, which means to "change one's mind." And this Greek word is in turn a poor translation of the original Hebrew word which means to "turn around." Hence we have here a word that has undergone a double degeneration. The question is, of course, whether this observation helps us very much. And then, too, the word "turn" does not really cast much light upon what we should do and where we are to turn. Earnest people who still cling to the idea that the words of an ancient tradition still have some wisdom in them and would like to make them profitable in their lives,—earnest people, in other words, who are concerned about the loss of real substance in our human life and therefore are looking for messages that gave weight and direction, stability and comfort to former generations,—usually proceed to interpret this word "to turn" in their own way. They make of it something in the nature of turning inward, returning to themselves. They say to themselves: "What we need in the hectic turmoil of our way of life is the healing quietness of reflection, we need to get away from things in a calm, creative way. We no longer know or come back to ourselves; today, however, I'm going to go back and commune with myself."

This therapeutic measure adopted by earnest people presents an interesting and constantly recurring phenomenon: When we have lost the real direction, when we no longer know where we are going, the Whither to which we are to turn, we turn to the *act* of turning, we simply "turn inward." When we no longer know what we should believe, we turn to the act of believing and simply cling to believing as an attitude. When we have lost the goal, we hold on to the act of "ever-striving endeavor," the aimless trudge of the Faustian wanderer.

And so, too, like these earnest people, we obscure and cut ourselves off from the real meaning of the Day of Repentance when we think of it merely as a time of reflection and meditation. Actually, the real purpose of this day is that we should reflect upon something, namely, upon the fact that our life is being suffocated by all kinds of things and that only one thing is needful: that we come to grips with ultimate reality. The rich fool in the New Testament had filled all his barns. He was a successful man and yet with all that he had gained he had lost the sustaining purpose of his life: he had failed to make his peace with God. Therefore in that night when God required of him his soul the whole product of his life slipped out of his fingers and his helpless hands were left groping in the void. A man may gain the whole world and lose his own soul. So the Day of Repentance does not ask us whether we are "standing on our own two feet" in life and whether in doing so we are cutting a good and stable figure. No, it asks *what* we are standing on with these two feet of ours. It could be that it only looks as if we were standing, when actually there is nothing underneath. This Day of Repentance asks us where our foundations are and it offers us these foundations.

The person who ignores this question and this offer cannot do anything else but interpret the Day of Repentance moralistically. For, naturally, we earnest people realize full well that we have failed in any number of ways and that we have not fulfilled what is required of us. So we think it quite proper that our turning inward should include reflection upon our obligations and shortcomings. We are quite ready to enter into judgment upon ourselves. Perhaps we conclude that our social order falls far short of being commensurate with what is demanded by our Western tradition. Perhaps we are horrified at the extent to which we have become subject to the fate of mass society and the degeneration of humanity that goes with it, and that a more than dubious future has already begun. We see work degenerating into numbing, stupefying labor, we see the destruction of recreation and leisure to the point where it becomes mere distraction and diversion from the real things of life, and we look for medicines against the symptoms of decay and deficiency.

And again it is the earnest people who believe that turning about and turning away from the evidences of decline and decay means reflecting upon the sustaining foundations of the Christian West and above all a regeneration of human dignity and its spiritual foundations in accord with the ideals of humanity in our tradition.

And here, too, of course, there is a thought that we must take seriously: this so-called Christian West of ours, along with its ideals of humanity, is only the result, I may even venture to say in conscious overstatement, is only the by-product of a very specific fact, and that is that our culture once came into contact with the Figure who gave it its stamp and bestowed upon it a certain, though questionable, right to call itself "Christian."

Because the Day of Repentance confronts us with the real goal and purpose of our turning about and therefore with this Figure, the real problem is this: In the long run can we keep the Christian West, if we lose this Figure who sustains, animates, and inspires it? Is it possible to hold on to certain Christian ideas about humanity, love of one's neighbor, and faith, if the figure of Christ himself disappears and we hold on our hands only copies of copies instead of the original? Is what we see still going on today anything more than the continuing revolving of a machine after the motor has long since been turned off and we can actually see that it has stopped? Can the principle of the "infinite value of the human soul" be upheld as long as we please to maintain it, if the very basis and reason for this value has disappeared, namely, that it has been purchased at great price, that the Son of God died for it, and that therefore it is under the protection of an eternal grace and goodness? Will not the worth of man become something that is merely used for what it is worth, will not man become a mere means of production, something to be used and consumed, if he is deprived of this relationship? (We need only to look to the East to see the end of this descent.)

Once more we are confronted with the theme of the Day of Repentance, namely, that everything depends upon the goal of our turning about, upon what we are turning to. If we do not want to be delivered over to this descent, which Grillparzer called the path from divinity to humanity to bestiality, then in our turning about everything depends upon our getting into the clear with this Figure who sustains our life. The Day of Repentance calls us away from a multitude of moralistic attempts to improve what needs to be improved, to the "one thing needful."

It is characteristic of the monumental monotony of the biblical message that it is constantly concentrating the whole theme of our life upon one point: Seek first the kingdom of God, then all the rest—humanity, social charity, community, the renewal of work—will be yours as well, then all these things will be added; they will emerge almost "incidentally." And conversely, if this one, real thing is missing, you may build great houses, but they will be built upon sand; you may fill your barns, but your hands will grope in the void; you may stand on your own two feet, but beneath you will yawn the bottomless abyss. Much would be gained if the Day of Repentance did no more than to open our eyes to this signature that sets the key for all that we are to do and do differently from what we have hitherto. The real decisions of our life are made before we add the key signature, before we begin to add up the items that constitute our life.

It would, of course, be wrong to see all this only in terms of sad, deadly seriousness. Revisions—and every repentance, every rightabout-face is, after all, a revision—are concerned with criticism and negation. And whether this rightabout-face turns out to be an act of negation depends solely upon where this turning is to lead us. Turning about in the Christian sense, however, does not mean that from now on we are going to do better; rather it means going home to him who had done all things well and forgiven all that was done wrong. It does not mean simply becoming a good person—who could seriously hope to achieve this! —but rather committing and entrusting ourselves to him who is good to us. Whether or not we come to terms with the ultimate, sustaining power of our life, whether or not we make our peace with that power does not depend upon our fulfilling certain conditions which would make it possible for this power to accept us, but solely upon what this power thinks of us, what its attitude toward us is. The Bible says with breathtaking simplicity that this ultimate power is good and friendly toward us. It says that God is willing to pay a tremendous price to pursue us down to the very depths of our life. It says that the Son of God does not merely call to us from the remote security of heaven, but that he came right down into our life, that he appears at the very place where we men are grappling with the powers of sin and suffering and death, and that he stands beside us and takes it all upon himself in order to be our brother.

If that is true—and the great ones of Christendom have always lived in the certainty that it is true, enduring the dark forces and dying in this certainty—then turning about is a joyful thing, because it means going back home.

> In every man there lives an image
> Of what he ought to be.
> As long as he is not that image,
> He ne'er at rest will be . . .

said Friedrich Rückert. It means going back home to what we were created and intended to be. We may enter, therefore, into that peace that is bestowed upon us when we become congruent with our design. But then that would mean the end of all critical negation; this would really be positive.

When the "lost son," whom we know from Jesus' parable, decided to go back home, he did so not because he was satiated and disgusted with the far country, not because his enchantment with being away from home and the orgies of his boundless freedom was followed by a moral hangover. It is true that the end of it was a pigsty, and this was the place for a very sad meditation in which his high flight into freedom ended in futility, and all his soaring turned out to be lost motion, and the question of what was the use of it all got a dusty answer. But there is no reason why this extreme fall into the depths should lead to his rehabilitation, no reason why new life should come out of this death. The last stop on the line, called "Pigsty," is only a symbol of the utter futility to which the lost son saw himself abandoned; it meant ending up in a void, in a prison with no exit.

What lifted him up was not his disgust with the far country, nor was it *horror vacui*, nor the hundred good intentions whose fecklessness he had tasted to excess. No, what gave him a new initiative was the recollection that his father's house was open to him, that the waiting lights were burning in its windows, and that there would come to meet him someone who loved him and would recognize him in all his rags as his own flesh and blood.

All this would surely be nothing but a beautiful tale, an unreal romance, if we did not know the one who tells us this story and vouches for it. Repentance is therefore not the negation of what lies behind us (or it is this negation only very incidentally), it is rather a joyful setting out for what lies ahead of us. To receive forgiveness means that our past is canceled and we have a new future. The Day of Repentance is the solemn promise that there is One who is waiting for us and that there is always a tomorrow. The one thing needful is also the one thing that is promised. Blessed are those who have a home, for they can come home.